THE LIFE OF A JESUS FOLLOWER

STOP LIVING FOR JESUS SO JESUS CAN LIVE THROUGH YOU

VANCE PITMAN

LifeWay Press®
Nashville, Tennessee

Editorial Team

Reid Patton
Bible Study Developer

Susan Hill
Production Editor

Jon Rodda
Art Director

Joel Polk
Editorial Team Leader

Brian Daniel
Manager, Short-Term Discipleship

Michael Kelley
Director, Discipleship and Groups Ministry

Ben Mandrell
President, LifeWay Christian Resources

Published by LifeWay Press® • © 2020 Vance Pitman
Used under License. All Rights Reserved.

No part of this book may be reproduced or transmitted in any form or by any means, electronic or mechanical, including photocopying and recording, or by any information storage or retrieval system, except as may be expressly permitted in writing by the publisher. Requests for permission should be addressed in writing to LifeWay Press®; One LifeWay Plaza; Nashville, TN 37234.

ISBN 978-1-5359-6083-0• Item 005815993

Dewey decimal classification: 248.84
Subject headings:: DISCIPLESHIP / JESUS CHRIST / CHRISTIAN LIFE

Unless indicated otherwise, Scripture quotations are taken from the New American Standard Bible® (NASB), Copyright © 1960, 1962, 1963, 1968, 1971, 1972, 1973, 1975, 1977, 1995 by The Lockman Foundation. Used by permission. www.lockman.org. Scripture quotations marked NLT are taken from the Holy Bible, New Living Translation, copyright ©1996, 2004, 2007, 2013, 2015 by Tyndale House Foundation. Used by permission of Tyndale House Publishers, Inc., Carol Stream, IL 60188. All rights reserved.

To order additional copies of this resource, write to LifeWay Resources Customer Service; One LifeWay Plaza; Nashville, TN 37234; fax 615-251-5933; call toll free 800-458-2772; order online at LifeWay.com; or email order-entry@lifeway.com.

Printed in the United States of America

Groups Ministry Publishing • LifeWay Resources • One LifeWay Plaza • Nashville, TN 37234 -

CONTENTS

ABOUT THE AUTHORS

VANCE PITMAN responded to God's call to Las Vegas, Nevada, in 2000, as a church plant from First Baptist Church in Woodstock, Georgia.

With a passion for God's kingdom, he had a vision to launch a church focused on joining in God's activity locally and globally. Thus, Hope Church was born in the fall of 2001. From a small group of eighteen adults meeting in a living room, Hope's fellowship has grown to more than 4000 people in small groups desiring to connect people to live the life of a Jesus follower. Vance has led Hope to understand that what God is doing is bigger than one church. Since its launch in 2001, Hope Church has sent hundreds out on mission, invested millions of dollars in God's global activity, and has commissioned dozens of new churches in the Western United States.

As a seasoned pastor and church planter, Vance speaks across the country and all over the world from the passion of his apostolic heart to inspire people to join in God's eternal, redemptive mission of making disciples and multiplying the church among every tribe, tongue, people, and nation.

Vance holds a Bachelor's Degree with a major in History and a minor in Business Management from the University of North Alabama, and a Master's Degree in Divinity from Mid-America Baptist Theological Seminary. He resides in Henderson, Nevada with his wife Kristie. He and Kristie are the proud parents of four children and two grandchildren.

INTRODUCTION

For years of my Christian journey, there were verses in the Bible that made no sense to me. Jesus said, "You will know the truth and the truth will set you free," but I didn't feel free. Jesus said, "Come to me … and I will give you rest," but I had no rest. For me, words like "freedom" and "rest" weren't part of my experience of following Jesus. I was trying hard to keep all the rules and regulations. The list of do's and don'ts seemed to grow daily. I was overwhelmed at how living for Jesus was just plain hard work, determination, and drudgery. Then I came to the greatest discovery of my life—Jesus didn't want me to live for Him; He desired to live His life through me. And His life is radically different!

As I began to pursue the life of Christ in the Gospels, I came to a conclusion. Jesus' life on earth revolved around three relationships. First, He walked in intimate fellowship with the Father. Everything He did, He did out of the overflow of intimacy with the Father. Second, He lived His life in community with His disciples. Sharing life with others was the outflow of His relationship with the Father. And third, He lived His life engaging and cultivating relationships with people who didn't know God at all. The kingdom expanded on the rails of relationships.

The more I consumed the pages of the Gospels, the more I realized every story in them could be dropped into one of three file drawers—Jesus and His relationship with the Father, Jesus and His relationship with the disciples, or Jesus and His relationship with unbelievers. Now if that's what His life looked like on earth, and my life is simply to be His life lived through me, what is my life to look like today? (1) A daily, intimate relationship with the Father, (2) a relationship of connecting in community with other believers, and (3) a cultivation of relationships with others who don't know Jesus to share Christ with them.

All believers should be able to lay this paradigm of following Jesus over their lives and examine to see if they're truly allowing His life to be manifest in them, or if they have settled for the cheap counterfeit of religion. The life of a Jesus follower revolves around three words: ABIDE, CONNECT, and SHARE. Abiding in Christ personally and daily, connecting in community in large groups and small groups, and sharing in the mission locally and globally, characterize the life of a Jesus follower.

As you begin this journey of walking through this Bible study exploring the simplicity of following Jesus, my prayer is that you'll find the same freedom and rest I've experienced in my own walk with the Lord as you learn to simply abide, connect, and share!

HOW TO USE THIS STUDY

This Bible-study book includes eight weeks of content for group and personal study.

GROUP SESSIONS

Regardless of what day of the week your group meets, each week of content begins with the group session. Each group session uses the following format to facilitate simple yet meaningful interaction among group members with God's Word and with the video teaching from pastor Vance Pitman

START. This page includes questions to get the conversation started and to introduce the video teaching.

WATCH. This page provides space to take notes on the video teaching.

DISCUSS. This page includes questions and statements that guide the group to respond to Vance's teaching andexplore relevant Bible passages.

PERSONAL STUDY

Each week provides five days of Bible study and learning activities for individual engagement between group sessions. The personal study revisits stories, Scriptures, and themes introduced in the video teaching, so participants can understand and apply them on a personal level. The days are numbered 1–5 to provide personal reading and activities for each day of the week, leaving two days off to worship with your church family and to meet as a small group. If your group meets on the same day as your worship gathering, use the extra day to reflect on what God is teaching you and to practice putting the biblical principles into action.

Each personal study includes the following three sections.

READ. This section lists the passages of Scripture you'll be studying that day. Take the time to read them slowly and prayerfully.

INTERACT. This section provides space for you to interact with what you just read using two questions. **1) What does the Bible say?** Many of us read the Bible so quickly we fail to recognize what the Bible is actually saying. This question is meant to help you gain understanding for what the Bible is communicating. **2) What do these passages teach me about following Jesus?** The whole Bible is a book about Jesus, so every passage teaches us about what it means to know and follow Him. This question is meant to help you begin to apply the Scriptures to your life.

REFLECT. This section contains a brief devotional thought along with a few questions to help you further understand, process, and apply the truths from the Bible.

DIGITAL RESOURCES

EBOOK. In addition to the print book, this book is also available as an ebook, which is immediately available after purchase in your LifeWay Reader library.

ENHANCED EBOOK In addition to the ebook, an enhanced ebook featuring integrated video assets such as a promotional video and session previews is also available after purchase in your LifeWay Reader library.

VIDEO SESSIONS. All eight video teaching sessions are available to rent or purchase as individual, downloadable sessions. Additionally, you'll find a group use bundle that gives your church a license to share digital video content with multiple groups in your church.

For these resources and more, visit LifeWay.com/JesusFollower

HOW DO I BEGIN A RELATIONSHIP WITH GOD?

At the very heart of this study is an intimate, growing relationship with God. Perhaps you're coming to this study asking, "How do I begin this relationship with God?" If that's you, take a moment and consider the following verses from the Bible carefully.

> Jesus answered and said to him, "Truly, truly, I say to you, unless one is born again he can't see the kingdom of God."
> **John 3:3**

According to the words of Jesus, there must be a point when a transformation takes place. In this passage, Jesus called it a new birth. In other words, every person must be spiritually made new on the inside by the power of God.

> For all have sinned and fall short of the glory of God.
> **Romans 3:23**

This new birth is necessary because of our sin. All have sinned. Every person ever born has sinned before God.

> The wages of sin is death...
> **Romans 6:23a**

The consequence of our sin (wage) is separation from God. Our sin makes a relationship impossible because of His holiness.

> But the free gift of God is eternal life through Jesus Christ our Lord.
> **Romans 6:23b**

> God demonstrates His own love toward us in that while we were yet sinners, Christ died for us.
> **Romans 5:8**

We were hopelessly separated from God by our sin. BUT because of His great love Jesus Christ took our sin debt upon Himself and died in our place.

> And He Himself bore our sins in His body on the cross, so that we might die to sin and live to righteousness; for by His wounds you were healed.
> **1 Peter 2:24**

Jesus took our sins and died for us in order to make it possible to enter into a relationship with God.

> But as many as received Him, to them He gave the right to become children of God, to those who believe in His name.
> **John 1:12**

Jesus died and made a relationship with God possible for everyone. But this relationship for each individual begins with a surrendered heart (deny self) and receiving of Jesus Christ as Savior and Lord.

> Whoever will call upon the name of the Lord will be saved.
> **Romans 10:13**

When a person realizes their great need for a Savior and trusts Jesus alone to be that Savior, then the relationship begins by simply calling upon Him. That is done by prayer. Simply cry out to God for forgiveness, and receive Jesus as the Lord and Savior of your life.

You can do that right now wherever you are. Stop and talk to God. Be honest with Him. Tell Him the desire of your heart, and trust Him to keep His promise. God knows your heart and isn't so concerned with the words as He is the attitude of your heart. The following is a suggested prayer:

> Lord Jesus, I need you. I realize I'm a sinner and separated from a relationship with You. I believe you died on a cross to pay my sin debt. I believe you rose from the dead after three days. I ask you to forgive me of my sin and I surrender the control of my life to you. Take control of my life, and make me the kind of person you want me to be.

Does this prayer express the desire of your heart? If so, pray to God right now and trust Him to change your life forever.

If you've made this wonderful decision, tell someone. Tell your small group leader, a Christian friend, or a pastor. They will rejoice with you and help you know what is best. Now you're truly a Jesus follower.

WEEK 1
BURDENED

Start

Welcome to week 1 of *The Life of a Jesus Follower*. Over the next eight sessions we're going to consider what it means to faithfully follow Jesus. Whether you've been following Jesus for decades, started following Him yesterday, or don't follow Jesus at all, you likely have some idea about what it means to follow Jesus, so let's begin by talking about those ideas.

> *How would you describe someone who follows Jesus? What should their life look like?*

> *What would you say is the goal of the Christian life?*

All of us have ideas about what it means to follow Jesus. We develop these ideas in a variety of ways—our family and friends, societal norms, and our church culture. The goal of this study is to help us cut through a cultural understanding of what it means to be a Christian and recover a biblical vision for what it means to follow Jesus.

To pursue that goal we're going to join Jesus in the Scriptures and learn from Him what it means to know and follow Him. So let's pause for a moment to pray and ask Jesus to bless our time as we pursue a deeper relationship with Him.

Ask someone to pray, then watch the video teaching.

Watch

Use this section to take notes as you watch video session 1.

Discuss

Use the following questions to facilitate a conversation with your group.

Vance began by saying we all have the tendency to make following Jesus about what we do or what we know. Why do we equate faithfulness with knowing and doing? Which tendency do you err towards most often?

Read 2 Corinthians 11:3. How do we miss the simplicity and purity of a relationship with Jesus when we reduce following Him to doing things for Him or knowing things about Him?

Following Jesus is about walking in the three relationships Jesus walked in (see John 15:5,12 and 17:18). What are these relationships, and where do we see them in the life of Jesus?

What can we learn about Jesus through relationships that we could never gain through knowing or doing?

Read John 13:34-35. How are the three relationships Jesus walked in interdependent?

What is the difference between living for Jesus and allowing Jesus to live in and through us?

We opened this session asking what it looks like to follow Jesus. How has your original answer changed in light of the video teaching?

Pause for a moment and pray together.
- *Praise God for who He is.*
- *Take hold of the freedom that comes from a relationship with Jesus.*
- *Expect the Spirit to work through the Scriptures and this study to grow your faith.*

After praying, remind the group to complete the five personal studies.

DAY 1
A JESUS FOLLOWER
EMBRACES RELATIONSHIPS

READ

Read the following passages slowly and carefully.

> 2 Corinthians 11:3
>
> Deuteronomy 6:5–9
>
> Matthew 22:36–40

INTERACT

Answer the following questions:

What does the Bible say?

What do these passages teach me about following Jesus?

REFLECT
Apply the teaching of Scripture to your life.

How did Jesus summarize the commands of God in Matthew 22?

We know the book of 2 Corinthians was originally a letter written from the apostle Paul to the church in the ancient city of Corinth. The church Paul had helped plant in that city was constantly under threat from internal struggles and strife. The Corinthians viewed information as their spiritual target, and they kept bickering with one another and creating division in their efforts to settle on the "correct" set of doctrines that would lead them to be faithful followers of Jesus.

In the middle of that immorality and strife, Paul wrote 2 Corinthians as a spiritual parent concerned for his children. And in that letter, he used a phrase that is both profoundly wise and incredibly relevant for Christians in our culture. Paul urged them to return to the simplicity and purity of devotion to Christ.

Consider what Paul said. Do those words describe your relationship with Jesus? Simple and pure? If not, why not?

We often prefer a superficial system of religion over a genuine relationship with Jesus because the superficial system is easier to control. We have a built-in desire to measure our performance whenever possible—not really because we want to excel, but because it makes it easy for us to say, "I may not be perfect, but I'm doing much better than those people." We've piled all these things on top of the simplicity and purity of simple devotion to Him.

That's a big problem. But thankfully, there's a solution. Love God and love others inside and outside of the church. Those two, straightforward, relationship driven commands are where we're going to spend the rest of our week.

Where do you feel you've lost the simplicity and purity of what it means to follow Jesus and turned your relationship into a list of do's and don'ts?

DAY 2
A JESUS FOLLOWER
ABIDES IN CHRIST

READ
Read the following passages slowly and carefully.

John 8:28-29

John 14:10-11

John 15:5,19

John 17:3

INTERACT
Answer the following questions:

What does the Bible say?

What do these passages teach me about following Jesus?

REFLECT
Apply the teaching of Scripture to your life.

The Gospels are filled with stories about Jesus and His relationship with God the Father. In this study, we'll use the word ABIDE to describe this relationship.

When you read through the Gospels, it's clear Jesus placed the priority of spending time with the Father above all else. In fact, it's important for us to understand that everything Jesus accomplished flowed from His intimate fellowship with the Father.

When the people of Jesus' day saw Him perform some great miracle, it was because of the Father working in and through Him. When they heard Jesus speak, it was the Father speaking through His Son. Jesus went so far as to say that He can don'thing without the father (John 5:19). Everything about Jesus' life was produced by the power of the Holy Spirit, which was born from His intimacy with the Father and overflowed into the world.

Jesus demonstrated what it looks like to live in moment-by-moment relationship with the Father. Once again, we see this pattern emerge through careful study of the Gospels. He often slipped away into the wilderness to spend time with the Father, just the two of them. Many times He stopped to settle in a garden or go up a mountain to be alone with God.

How much more should the same thing be true of us? The ultimate pursuit of Jesus's life was an intimate love relationship with God the Father. What was true in Jesus's life will be true in our lives as we faithfully follow Him. We must pursue intimacy with the Father by abiding in Christ both personally and daily.

What do we gain by abiding in Christ?

How are you currently seeking to abide in Christ personally and daily?

If Jesus believed that apart from an intimate love relationship with Father He could do nothing, why do we often view it as something that is optional to faithfully follow Him?

DAY 3
A JESUS FOLLOWER
CONNECTS WITH
OTHER BELIEVERS

READ
Read the following passages slowly and carefully.

> John 1:35-51
>
> Mark 4:35-41
>
> Luke 9:12-27

INTERACT
Answer the following questions:

What does the Bible say?

What do these passages teach me about following Jesus?

REFLECT
Apply the teaching of Scripture to your life.

The Gospels are filled with stories of Jesus actively and intentionally cultivating relationships with His disciples. And there are many of these stories. In this study, we'll use the word CONNECT to describe Jesus' relationship with His disciples and our relationship with other followers of Jesus.

Jesus started by calling His disciples away from their old lives so they could join Him in doing the work of His kingdom. Jesus prayed with His disciples. He taught them, cared for them, challenged them, and walked with each of them through the ups and downs of life.

Jesus devoted time, energy, and passion to His relationships with twelve men. He identified them and invited them to walk alongside Him (John 1:35–51). Jesus joined the disciples on what was supposed to be a quick sail across the Sea of Galilee—and He used the resulting storm to teach them about the power of faith in difficult times (Mark 4:35–41). Jesus challenged His disciples to feed a crowd of more than 5,000 people and then challenged them to trust God in every circumstance by using only five loaves and two fish to provide a feast for everyone (Luke 9:12–27).

The Gospels serve as historical records of the relationship and fellowship that existed between Jesus and His friends. Jesus poured His life into the disciples. Jesus' intimate relationship with the Father spilled into intentional relationships with His disciples.

Why are relationships with other Christians nonnegotiable for Jesus followers?

What do we gain by investing in relationships with other Jesus followers?

How are you currently investing in your relationships with other Jesus followers?

DAY 4
A JESUS FOLLOWER
SHARES WITH THE WORLD

READ
Read the following passages slowly and carefully.

> John 3:1-17
>
> John 4:7-29
>
> Luke 19:1-10
>
> Matthew 9:9-13

INTERACT
Answer the following questions:

What does the Bible say?

What do these passages teach me about following Jesus?

REFLECT

Apply the teaching of Scripture to your life.

What do you notice about the relationships Jesus cultivated with people who didn't yet follow Him?

The Gospels are filled with stories of Jesus pursuing relationships with the world—meaning, with those who didn't know God. As you journey through the Gospels, you'll read story after story of Jesus seeking out people who were in desperate need of His saving grace. Throughout this study, we'll use the word SHARE to describe Jesus' relationship with the world.

The religious leaders accused Jesus of being a friend of sinners because He joined the hated tax collectors for a meal (Matt. 9:10–12). The tax collector named Zacchaeus welcomed Jesus into his home (Luke 19:1–10). Whether it's those lost in the darkness of religion such as Nicodemus, or those trapped in the seduction of sexual sin such as the Samaritan woman— Jesus is constantly looking to engage with those who are far from God to bring to them the life-changing message of the gospel.

One of the key patterns of Jesus' life was building intentional, engaging, loving relationships with people who were far from God, so He could lead them back to God. If we seek to faithfully follow Jesus, we'll pursue the same kind of relationships Jesus pursued with the world.

What do we gain by investing in relationships with people outside of our faith?

How are you currently developing relationships with people who don't know Jesus?

DAY 5
A JESUS FOLLOWER
EMBRACES RELATIONSHIPS

READ
Read the following passage slowly and carefully.

John 13:34-35

INTERACT
Answer the following questions:

What does the Bible say?

What does the passage teach me about following Jesus?

REFLECT
Apply the teaching of Scripture to your life.

Over the next seven weeks of this study, we'll take a deeper look at the three relationships
we've thought about this week. But here at the end of this first week, there's one crucial truth
we need to think more deeply about. All three of these relationships are interdependent.
Listen to the way Jesus describes it in John's Gospel:

> A new commandment I give to you, that you love one
> another, even as I have loved you [Abide], that you also love
> one another [Connect]. By this all men will know [Share]
> that you're My disciples, if you've love for one another.
> **John 13:34-35**

Do you see how Jesus powerfully wove all three relationships together? It's out of the overflow of our love relationship with Him that God manifests through us the kind of love He
desires us to have for one another. Then those relationships become the greatest platform we
have to authenticate the gospel to this world. It takes all three to function.

In Jesus' day, the defining mark of a disciple was the relationship they enjoyed with the
one they were following. The same is true in our day. Being a follower of Jesus isn't simply
conforming to a system of moral behavior, nor is it merely comprehending a set of doctrinal
truths. Following Jesus is first and foremost a relationship. In fact, it's all about relationships.

*How has your understanding of what it means to follow Jesus changed as you
studied Scripture this week?*

*Where do you see the greatest opportunity for Jesus to work in your life
through this study?*

WEEK 2
ABIDE
I'M IN A RELATIONSHIP WITH GOD

Start

Welcome to week 2 of *The Life of a Jesus Follower*.

Last week, you were introduced to the idea that following Jesus is all about relationships. How did this challenge the way you've thought about faith before? How did it encourage you?

Outside of your family, what is the first relationship you remember having?

As we're continuing to work through what it means to faithfully follow Jesus, we need to start where Jesus started—a relationship with God. A love relationship with the Father is the primary relationship in the life of a Jesus follower.

When did you first realize you needed a relationship with God?

This week and next week, we'll be taking a closer look at our relationship with the Father. We'll begin where Jesus began—with an invitation to know God through a relationship with Him.

Ask someone to pray, then watch the video teaching.

Watch

Use this section to take notes as you watch video session 2.

Discuss

Use the following questions to facilitate a conversation with your group.

Read Mark 3:13-14

How does knowing that Jesus summons (or invites you) to follow Him change the way you think about your relationship with Him?

According to verse 14, why did Jesus invite us to follow Him? Why would Mark include that detail?

Would you say you know Jesus in the way Vance described in this session?

When have you made your relationship with Jesus more about doing things for Him rather than being with Him?

If the objective of the Christian life is to know God and spend time with Him, why do we find it hard to carve out daily time with God?

What barriers in your schedule keep you from spending time alone with God? How could you overcome those barriers?

If you've already developed the habit of regularly spending time alone with God, share how that relationship with Jesus has overflowed into other areas of your life.

Pause for a moment, and pray together.
- Embrace God's invitation to follow Him in relationship.
- Thank Jesus for seeking a relationship with you.
- Ask the Spirit to help you identify barriers in your life that keep you from spending time with Him.

After praying, remind the group to complete the five personal studies.

DAY 1
A JESUS FOLLOWER
IS LOVED BY GOD

READ
Read the following passages slowly and carefully.

1 John 3:1

1 John 4:8-10

John 15:9

Romans 5:8

Romans 8:35-39

INTERACT
Answer the following questions:

What does the Bible say?

What does the passage teach me about following Jesus?

REFLECT
Apply the teaching of Scripture to your life.

The Bible says much about the love of God towards His children. His love for us is great, never-ending, unchanging, beyond knowledge and understanding. Because God's love for us is unchanging, He can't love us any more or any less than He does right now. On good days, bad days, and every day in between—at every moment in time—God loves you exactly as much as He does today because His love for you isn't rooted in your performance for Him but in your position in Christ.

As followers of Jesus, you share in the perfect, eternal, unchanging love that has existed between the Father and Son for eternity (John 15:9). You are loved and accepted as a child of the Father, and there's nothing you can do to change it because God's love comes to you through grace—the unmerited favor of God. The cross is a public demonstration of God's immense love for you.

On the cross, while you were a sinner, Jesus died *for you*. His sacrifice on your behalf satisfied God's judgment against your sin and extended God's love and mercy to you. What's more, if you know and follow Jesus, you've been invited into a loving relationship with the Father that lasts forever. To abide in God's love is to remain in and enjoy God's love at all times. No matter what happens, nothing can change God's love for you.

Would you say that you're abiding in God's love right now? If not, why not?

When are you most tempted to doubt God's love for you?

Pick one verse from the previous page, and use that verse to spend a few minutes praying and thanking God for His love for you.

DAY 2
A JESUS FOLLOWER
HAS BEEN CHANGED BY GOD

READ

Read the following passages slowly and carefully.

Ephesians 1:3-14

Ephesians 2:4-10

INTERACT

Answer the following questions:

What does the Bible say?

What does the passage teach me about following Jesus?

REFLECT
Apply the teaching of Scripture to your life.

The moment people become aware of God's love for them and surrender by turning from their sin and placing their faith in Christ (becoming Jesus followers) those people are changed forever. The Bible often speaks of the spiritual blessings God lavished upon us.

In the space below, write down some of those blessings God gives Christians based on the previous verses.

People who follow Jesus are blessed, chosen, holy, adopted, redeemed, forgiven, filled with the Holy Spirit, created for good works, and given access to Him to name a few of the benefits described in these verses. The trouble is many of these things are "spiritual" truths that can't be seen. The Christian life is learning to live out here on earth what is already true about you before God. Even though these blessings are internal, nothing you do can add to or take away from these blessings. They're finished works in the Father's eyes. It's all a work of God through His wonderful grace

Consider how you think about yourself. What needs to change for you to see yourself the way God sees you?

DAY 3
A JESUS FOLLOWER
PURSUES GOD

READ
Read the following passages slowly and carefully.

> Exodus 33:13-18
>
> Psalm 63:1-3
>
> Philippians 3:7-14

INTERACT
Answer the following questions:

What does the Bible say?

What does the passage teach me about following Jesus?

REFLECT
Apply the teaching of Scripture to your life.

What did Moses, David, and Paul all have in common?

People come to know God personally the moment they surrender to Him by faith and receive Jesus as the Lord and Savior of their life. But salvation is only the beginning. Because God is infinite, we'll never exhaust the riches of who He is. Even though we'll never know God fully, we can know Him truly. To do this, we must pursue a relationship with the Father, which is a life-long pursuit.

Deep in the soul of a Jesus follower is a hunger to know God more. The more you come to know God, the more you'll desire Him. He invites you to know Him. He desires you to know Him. There's no higher pursuit in life than to pursue God through Jesus Christ.

Do you hunger and desire to know God like that? Why or why not?
What distracts you from Him?

Was there a time in your life when you hungered for God more than you do now? If so, what changed, and what steps do you need to take today to begin to pursue God like that again?

DAY 4
A JESUS FOLLOWER
MEETS WITH GOD

READ
Read the following passages slowly and carefully.

John 15:1-5

Luke 10:38-42

INTERACT
Answer the following questions:

What does the Bible say?

What does the passage teach me about following Jesus?

REFLECT
Apply the teaching of Scripture to your life.

Based on these passages, is God more interested in what we can do for Him or in the time we spend with Him?

The Christian life isn't about what we can do for God. It's not about how many church services we attend, how much we give, or how many people we help. It's about an intimate, growing relationship that involves spending time with Jesus.

The word "abide" isn't likely a word you use very regularly. Another word to translate the same word is "remain." Jesus is inviting you to remain with Him—to stick with Him. This isn't an invitation to do something for Him but to be with Him. Jesus commended Mary for wanting to simply sit at His feet and spend time with Him. When you busy yourself like Martha, you miss the joy Mary found in remaining at Jesus' feet. When you remain in Jesus, you're allowing Him to fill you up, so the rest of your life comes out of the overflow of the time you spent meeting with Jesus.

The God of the universe wants to spend time with you. It's a daily invitation to be with Him. There's no more important aspect of the Christian life than regular time set apart to simply be with Him. Everything in your life will flow out of this. Remember, God has called you to a loving relationship before anything else.

Is your Christian life characterized by activity or intimacy?

How is working through this study increasing your desire to have regular, unhurried time alone with God?

DAY 5
A JESUS FOLLOWER
TALKS TO GOD

READ

Read the following passages slowly and carefully.

> Luke 18:1-8
>
> John 14:13-14
>
> John 15:7

INTERACT

Answer the following questions:

What does the Bible say?

What does the passage teach me about following Jesus?

REFLECT
Apply the teaching of Scripture to your life.

You can't be close to someone you never speak to. Your relationship with God is the same way. You can't be close to God and never talk to Him. We hear from God in the Bible, and we converse with God in prayer.

Prayer is a relationship, not a religious exercise; it's a two-way conversation. The ear of God hears the prayers of His children; He listens and uses our prayers to conform us to His character. This is why we pray in Jesus' name. To pray in Jesus' name simply means to pray consistently with His character and according to His will. And we know His character and will through the Bible. In John 15:7, Jesus says, "If ... my Words abide in you, ask." The Bible and prayer go hand in hand.

Is your prayer life characterized by communion with God or merely a religious exercise? What's the difference between those two approaches?

Do you spend more time listening or talking in prayer?

Are your prayers a demonstration of following Jesus or of wanting Him to follow you?

If you find that you struggle in prayer, consider praying with a Bible open in front of you. The Bible is God talking to you, but it can also serve as your guide in what to say to Him. When we pray the words of Scripture, we know we're praying according to His will. The Psalms are a great place to start. Many of the 150 Psalms are prayers David and others offered to God. They contain a variety of prayers for every imaginable occasion and will provide a much-needed boost to your prayer life.

WEEK 3
ABIDE
SPENDING TIME WITH GOD

Start

Welcome to week 3 of *The Life of a Jesus Follower.*

> *Have you found working through the personal studies helpful in cultivating time alone with God? If so, share one insight you've gained over the last two weeks.*

> *Who is the person you spend the most time with? What do you love about that person?*

> *What is something surprising you've learned about this person as you've gotten to know them?*

If you're married, you likely know and appreciate your spouse now in a way you couldn't when you were just dating. Why? Over time, your relationship has grown and developed through intimacy.

Last week we saw that the primary relationship of a Jesus follower is their relationship with God. This week we're going to focus on how we develop that relationship. Like all relationships, we learn to love and appreciate God as we spend time with Him.

Ask someone to pray, then watch the video teaching.

Watch

Use this section to take notes as you watch video session 3.

Discuss

Use the following questions to facilitate a conversation with your group.

Why is it so easy for even mature Jesus followers to confuse spiritual activity for spiritual maturity? When have you done this?

In this session, Vance shared some questions his mentor asked him:
- *Does a Christian want to sin?*
- *Does a Christian have to sin?*

How would you've answered these questions before watching this session? How has your answer changed in light of what you heard?

Read 1 Corinthians 10:13 and 2 Peter 1:3 . What options does a Christian have when confronted with sin?

Read John 14:15 & 21. How is our willingness to sin related to our love for God? How have you found this to be true in your own life?

How have pride and self-sufficiency kept you from pursuing God? Is this happening in your life right now?

Read James 4:6. Why does our humility grow in proportion to our love for God?

How can we be committed to spending time with God without it becoming just another activity we do for God?

Pause for a moment and pray together.
- *Ask God for a renewed commitment to Him.*
- *Confess your pride and your need for God to sustain you.*
- *Pray for greater grace as you depend upon God personally and daily.*

After praying, remind the group to complete the five personal studies.

DAY 1
A JESUS FOLLOWER
KNOWS GOD

READ
Read the following passages slowly and carefully.

> **Exodus 3:1-6**
>
> **Exodus 3: 13-15**

INTERACT
Answer the following questions:

What does the Bible say?

What does the passage teach me about following Jesus?

REFLECT
Apply the teaching of Scripture to your life.

To know God more intimately is the greatest pursuit in life. The amazing truth is that God wants you to know Him more. We know this because the Bible is full of accounts where God reveals Himself in specific ways to individuals. He may not speak to you from a burning bush as He did with Moses, but God continues to reveal Himself to us today through His Word.

God wants you to know Him, and He has given us the Bible to know Him. We don't read the Bible to be an ace at Bible trivia but to know the God behind the Bible. God desires we have intimate encounters with Him in our daily lives, so that we not only know about Him, but we know who He is personally.

Below is a list of verses in which God reveals Himself. Beside each verse, write the name, title, or description of God that each verse reveals. Before you do this exercise, stop and prayerfully ask God for you to not merely know about Him, but for you to know Him intimately as He reveals Himself to you. The first one is done for you.

Genesis 17:1 *God Almighty*	*Habakkuk 3:18-19*
Isaiah 47:4	*1 Chronicles 29:11-12*
Genesis 22:14	*Psalm 32:7*
Genesis 16:13	*John 10:11*
Jeremiah 10:12	*Isaiah 40:28-31*
Psalm 48:14	*Colossians 3:4*
Lamentations 3:25	*Isaiah 41:10*
Psalm 33:20	*Revelation 19:11,16*
Hosea 13:4	
Isaiah 9:6	

DAY 2
A JESUS FOLLOWER
LOVES GOD

READ
Read the following passages slowly and carefully.

> 1 John 4:19
>
> Joshua 22:5
>
> Deuteronomy 6:5
>
> Matthew 22:37

INTERACT
Answer the following questions:

What does the Bible say?

What does the passage teach me about following Jesus?

REFLECT
Apply the teaching of Scripture to your life.

We're only able to love God because He first loved us. Our love for God is only in response to His great love for us. As we've said several times throughout our time together, a love relationship with God is at the very heart of what it means to follow Jesus. Everything in our life is dependent upon the quality of our love relationship with Him.

Most of our difficulties in the Christian life can be traced back to a love problem. Love for God, like faith, doesn't come naturally. It's only possible as God reveals Himself to us, and we choose to respond to Him lovingly. If this isn't right, nothing else will be right, and this is why Jesus believed loving God was the greatest commandment of all.

Loving God isn't a suggestion; it's a command that expresses God's desire for us. He desires that we love Him to the very core of our beings (heart). He desires that we love Him with all of our emotions (soul). He desires that we love Him with all of our energy (strength). He desires that we'll fully choose to love Him (mind). The God of all creation lacks nothing, yet He chooses to love us, and He wants our love in return. Because we're the only creatures created in God's image, we're the only created beings who have the capacity to love Him like that. We can love God in an intelligent, emotional, willing, and active way.

Why should God's love for you motivate your love for Him?

Do you willingly choose to love God in response to His great love, or is it dependent upon circumstances? Why should we love God independently of our circumstances?

God desires that we love Him sincerely, passionately, willingly, and actively. Love for Him doesn't come naturally; it deepens and develops as we know Him more. The more we know Him, the more we love Him.

DAY 3
A JESUS FOLLOWER
OBEYS GOD

READ
Read the following passages slowly and carefully.

John 4:34

John 14:15,23-24,31

1 Samuel 15:22

1 John 2:3-5

INTERACT
Answer the following questions:

What does the Bible say?

What does the passage teach me about following Jesus?

REFLECT
Apply the teaching of Scripture to your life.

The personal studies in this week build upon one another. On the first day, we saw that Jesus followers know God. Those who know God will love God, which we thought about on the previous day. Those who know and love God will also obey God.

Following Jesus is impossible without obedience. At its core, obedience is simply the life of Jesus in me, being lived through me. According to Jesus, obedience to Him is an outward expression of love (John 14:15, 24a). Therefore, an obedience problem is a love problem. We'll never obey Christ perfectly this side of heaven, but a characteristic of true Jesus followers is a desire to obey God (1 John 2:3-5).

If a Christian, by definition, is a "little Christ," then we should look more and more like Jesus. That raises the question, how did Jesus live?

Jesus lived in complete obedience to God. As Jesus lives through us, it will look the same. We don't obey God in order to get things from God. We obey God because we love God. Understanding this distinction is critical for following Jesus. Obedience doesn't earn God's love for us, it provides evidence of our love for God. Remember Jesus promised He would reveal Himself to those who obey (14:21, 23). When He reveals Himself in response to obedience, the result will always be deeper love for Him.

> *What is the difference between obeying out of duty and obeying out of love? Which most often describes your obedience?*

> *What have you learned about God through obeying Him?*

> *Is there an area where you're not obeying God and need to seek forgiveness? If so, pray and confess your sin now.*

DAY 4
A JESUS FOLLOWER
IS DEPENDENT ON GOD

READ
Read the following passages slowly and carefully.

> John 15:5
>
> Galatians 2:20
>
> 1 Corinthians 15:10
>
> Luke 18:9-14

INTERACT
Answer the following questions:

What does the Bible say?

What does the passage teach me about following Jesus?

REFLECT
Apply the teaching of Scripture to your life.

According to the previous verses: What can we do on our own apart from God?

Which statement in these verses is most difficult for you?

These verses allow no room for pride. Jesus followers recognize their total dependence upon God to accomplish anything of eternal value. Jesus says we can do nothing apart from Him. Paul says we're crucified with Christ. A dead man can't accomplish much unless someone lives through Him.

Jesus is life. He tells us in John 15:5 that our relationship to Him is like a vine and a branch. We (the branch) are totally dependent upon Him (the vine) for strength, energy, and nourishment in order to bear fruit in our lives. Fruit's simply the life of Jesus in us being lived through us. The Christian life isn't about us living for Jesus; the Christian life is about Jesus living His life in and through us out of the overflow of our abiding in Him. The Christian life isn't about overworking or about what we can do for God. It's about being so intimately connected to Him that He lives His life out and accomplishes His purposes through us. The Christian life isn't about becoming a better version of ourselves. It's about dying to ourselves so that Christ may live through us. The key is a relationship with a person—Jesus Christ.

Where in life are you trying to live for Jesus instead of allowing Jesus to live through you?

DAY 5
A JESUS FOLLOWER
ENJOYS GOD

READ
Read the following passages slowly and carefully.

Philippians 4:4

Psalm 16:11

Acts 16:23-25

INTERACT
Answer the following questions:

What does the Bible say?

What does the passage teach me about following Jesus?

REFLECT
Apply the teaching of Scripture to your life.

To know God is to enjoy God. In fact, The Westminster Catechism said that the chief end of man (the goal of life) is to know God and enjoy Him forever. You were created to delight in God forever. The life of a Jesus follower should be marked with joy because God is the ultimate source of deep abiding joy.

The enjoyment we find in God isn't a happiness dependent on circumstances but a joy we find only in God's presence, in communion with Him (Ps. 16:11). This is why Paul and Silas enjoyed God in a jail cell. Their joy was not determined by circumstance, but by a relationship with the living God. .

True, abiding joy is only found in an intimate, love relationship with Jesus. In John 15:11, Jesus tells us that abiding in Him allows us to experience the joy Christ has in us. This joy is independent of external circumstances. Following Jesus isn't a journey of drudgery, but the pathway to full abiding joy. The type of joy found in Jesus manifests itself in authentic praise, thankful attitudes, and a Christlike contentment that will be obvious to all.

Would you say that your life following Jesus is filled with joy? Why or why not?

What does it communicate to the world about following Jesus if Christians aren't joyful people?

When have you experienced contentment and joy despite trying circumstances?

WEEK 4
CONNECT
I BELONG

Start

Welcome to week 4 of *The Life of a Jesus Follower*. For the next two weeks we'll be focusing on our second key word CONNECT, which describes our fellowship with other followers of Jesus.

What is your biggest takeaway from the ABIDE section of our study?

Being a Jesus follower begins with a relationship with God, this was the focus of the last two weeks. The next two sessions are built on the truth that being a Jesus follower isn't just about a relationship with God. From the very beginning, people were created for community (Gen. 2:18).

If we're walking in a relationship with God, we'll naturally desire to be in relationships with other Jesus followers. Jesus modeled this for us by building His ministry through a close-knit group of disciples. His example shows us we'll never experience the best God has for us apart from relationship with others.

What are some ways knowing other Christians has strengthened your faith?

Ask someone to pray, then watch the video teaching.

Watch

Use this section to take notes as you watch video session 4.

Discuss

Use the following questions to facilitate a conversation with your group.

Vance taught that God created us for community. How do the people you know demonstrate a natural desire for relationship?

Why should a right relationship with God compel us to have deep relationships with other Christians?

Read Hebrews 10:24-35. Have you ever heard someone say they love Jesus, but they don't like the church? Why is this not something a follower of Jesus can rightly believe?

Read John 1:12 and Romans 8:15-16. How does the image of a family help us better understand our connection to other Christians?

Vance said that church isn't "an event you attend but a family to which you belong." How does this statement challenge the way we often think about the church?

Outside of a group like this, how are you currently connecting with your brothers and sisters in Christ?

What are some ways you could grow and strengthen your relationships with other Jesus followers?

Pause for a moment and pray together.
- Thank God for the blessing of relationships.
- Ask that He would strengthen the relationships in your Christian community.
- Pray for unity in the Spirit and a bond of peace (Eph. 4:4).

After praying, remind the group to complete the five personal studies.

DAY 1
JESUS FOLLOWERS
CONNECT WITH ONE ANOTHER

READ

Read the following passages slowly and carefully.

John 1:12

John 17:17,20-23

Romans 8:16-17

Luke 8:19-21

INTERACT

Answer the following questions:

What does the Bible say?

What does the passage teach me about following Jesus?

REFLECT
Apply the teaching of Scripture to your life.

What is the unique connection that binds believers together?

Jesus followers share a unique connection to one another that we won't see in relationships among those who haven't yet believed. Jesus gives insight regarding the depth of that connection in John 17. There is a unity that exists exclusively among believers. John compared this supernatural connection to the relationship that has existed for all of eternity between the Father and the Son.

The Father and the Son share an eternal, intimate, and vibrant relationship that our human minds can't fully grasp. Likewise, because of our relationship with God, we've entered into a family relationship with God Himself. As God's children, we're connected to all other Christians intimately and eternally. This is why Jesus was able to say that those who follow Him are His true family. This also helps us understand that to be in a relationship with Jesus, you must also be in a relationship with the members of His family.

What value do you place on your spiritual family?

How can you be more connected to God's family?

Write out a prayer to God thanking Him for your spiritual family.

DAY 2
JESUS FOLLOWERS
LOVE ONE ANOTHER

READ

Read the following passages slowly and carefully.

> John 13:34-35
>
> John 15:1-17
>
> 1 John 4:12

INTERACT

Answer the following questions:

What does the Bible say?

What does the passage teach me about following Jesus?

REFLECT
Apply the teaching of Scripture to your life.

What are the two primary commandments in John 15? Why does this matter?

Jesus followers are in a relationship with God Himself. As a result, all Jesus followers share an intimate connection with one another. The greatest indicator of the state of our relationship with Jesus is our love for one another. The two primary commands in John 15 are "abide in me" and "love one another." It's impossible to truly love God and not love one another. The two go hand in hand. The fruit of intimacy with Christ isn't isolation from others but rather connection with one another.

Love for one another isn't a suggestion; it's a command of Jesus. Therefore, our connection extends beyond emotion. Emotions may accompany our love for others, but genuine love for one another is characterized by positive action (John 15:13). Genuine love always moves Jesus followers to act, not merely "feel" love toward one another. Christ demonstrated this as His love for us moved Him to the cross. Our love for each other motivates us to self-sacrifice and service towards others in the family of God.

What things in your life take priority over the relationships God has given you?

How do you demonstrate love for other Christians?

Ask God to reveal your lack of love for other believers. Ask Him to show you how to love others biblically and to give you the strength to love like He loves you.

DAY 3
JESUS FOLLOWERS
HAVE GENUINE FELLOWSHIP

READ

Read the following passage slowly and carefully.

1 John 1:1-7

INTERACT

Answer the following questions:

What does the Bible say?

What does the passage teach me about following Jesus?

REFLECT
Apply the teaching of Scripture to your life.

Reread the verses and notice the number of times John used the word "fellowship." What is necessary before true fellowship can take place?

If you grew up in church, you're probably familiar with the way churches use the word "fellowship." Typically, it means a meal together at the church. The meal may even take place in the "fellowship hall." But the word "fellowship" is greatly misunderstood in the church today. Prayerfully, over the next two days, God will give us greater understanding of true biblical fellowship.

The Greek word the biblical authors most often use for "fellowship" literally means "to share in the life of another." The word means the fullest possible partnership and relationship with God and other believers. The kind of fellowship with God that the Scriptures call us to only comes from a personal encounter with the living Christ and surrendering to Him as Lord of our lives. It's an intimate love relationship with God that grows sweeter each day as we follow Jesus. However, this type of fellowship relationship doesn't stop with God. Jesus followers have this type of relationship with one another as well.

In today's reading the apostle John wrote about his fellowship with God. John had an experiential knowledge of Jesus. This is the way we know God—in a real, intimate, and experiential way. This relationship deepens each day we follow Jesus.

John proclaimed Jesus so others would believe and come to know Him the way he did. The result would be fellowship with God and other believers. In verses 3-4, John says when we see others come into fellowship with God, our joy is made complete by seeing the cleansing work of Jesus in the life of someone else.

How would you describe your fellowship relationship with other believers?

Do you value your fellowship with other believers as highly as you value your fellowship with God?

DAY 4
JESUS FOLLOWERS
HAVE GENUINE FELLOWSHIP PT. 2

READ
Read the following passages slowly and carefully.

> 1 John 1:7
>
> 1 John 2:9-11
>
> 1 John 3:10,14-17
>
> 1 John 4:7-8,20-21
>
> 1 John 5:1-2

INTERACT
Answer the following questions:

What does the Bible say?

What does the passage teach me about following Jesus?

REFLECT
Apply the teaching of Scripture to your life.

Read the previous verses again and notice the words brother(s) and love.

In the space below, write in your own words the interdependence between our fellowship relationship with God and our fellowship relationship with one another.

You can't be in fellowship with God and not walk in fellowship with one another. The two are interdependent. The Scriptures make clear your relationships with other believers are an expression of your relationship with God. John even says those who claim fellowship with God and don't love their brothers and sisters are liars. In other words, it's easy to profess with your mouth a relationship with God. How we relate to one another will prove or disprove the validity of that claim. It's impossible to love and have fellowship with a God we can't see and not love other believers whom we can see.

True fellowship with others means loving others the same way Jesus loved us—by laying down our lives for the good of one another. Jesus followers love with a sanctifying love by being as committed to the spiritual growth of others as we're to our own.

It's impossible to be in fellowship with God and not walk in godly fellowship with one another. The two are interdependent. This isn't a burdensome truth but one that John says will make our joy complete!

What does your love for other believers reveal about your relationship with God?

Ask God to continue to give you better understanding of this truth and of specific ways to live it out this week.

DAY 5
JESUS FOLLOWERS
SERVE ONE ANOTHER

READ

Read the following passages slowly and carefully.

> John 13:1-17
>
> Philippians 2:1-11

INTERACT

Answer the following questions:

What does the Bible say?

What does the passage teach me about following Jesus?

REFLECT
Apply the teaching of Scripture to your life.

What was the washing of the disciples' feet an expression of based on John 13?

Jesus was a servant. As He lives through you, you'll become a servant as well. In the Jewish culture, the task of washing feet was such a demeaning task that Jewish servants weren't required to carry it out. Only non-Jewish servants were expected to stoop to this level of humiliation. The disciples likely considered the task someone else's responsibility and thus the task went undone. They were too busy arguing about who was the greatest (Luke 22:24).

As an expression of His infinite love, the God of the universe took a towel and the basin, and washed the filth of the world from the feet of His disciples. He commands us to do the same (v. 14). If you're following Jesus you're not above your master. No act of service you could ever perform could surpass the humiliating act of Jesus being mocked, beaten, forced to carry a cross, and publicly executed. True blessing is found when you embrace humility and serve one another in love.

What areas of service do you shy away from because they're else's responsibility?

Are there areas of service you consider beneath you?

Whose feet might God be calling you to wash by performing a sacrificial act of timely service?

WEEK 5
CONNECT
LIFE IN COMMUNITY

Start

Welcome to week 5 of *The Life of a Jesus Follower*. Last week we began looking deeper into our relationships with other Jesus followers. This week we'll continue to talk about what it means to CONNECT with your brothers and sisters in Christ.

What was your biggest takeaway from last week's personal study?

What would you say is the goal of the Christian life?

When we were born into a relationship with God, we were also given a relationship with God's family—the church. While our culture increasingly devalues church attendance, we must be more committed to God's family in the church.

At its core, Christianity is about having a relationship with God that extends to our relationships with others inside and outside of the church. In this session, we're going to take a look at the first Christian community in the book of Acts and see that for the early church living in community was absolutely essential.

Ask someone to pray, then watch the video teaching.

Watch

Use this section to take notes as you watch video session 5.

Discuss

Use the following questions to facilitate a conversation with your group.

Read Acts 2:42-47.

How did the first Christian community care for and support one another?

How do our relationships with other Christians deepen our relationship with God? What would you not know about God without other Jesus followers?

The word the Bible uses for fellowship means "to join in the life of another person." Why is connecting beyond a once a week Bible study essential?

Scripture contains 40 "one another" commands (Mark 9:50; Rom.12:16; Eph. 4:32; 1 Thess. 5:11; Jas. 5:9). Why must we have relationships with other Christians to faithfully follow Jesus?

How did the early believers support and celebrate with each other? Why is community essential in both good and bad circumstances?

In the first century, many people came to faith by seeing relationships in the church. How is God using our relationships with each other to make a tangible impact in the world around us?

The Bible describes the church as a body. In what ways does the church demonstrate to the world that Jesus is real?

Pause for a moment and pray together.
- *Commit to walking together through the ups and downs of life.*
- *Ask for the gift of fulfilling the "one another" commands to each other.*
- *Pray that God would use this community to make His love visible in the world.*

After praying, remind the group to complete the five personal studies.

DAY 1
JESUS FOLLOWERS
PRAY FOR ONE ANOTHER

READ
Read the following passage slowly and carefully.

John 17:9-26

INTERACT
Answer the following questions:

What does the Bible say?

What does the passage teach me about following Jesus?

REFLECT
Apply the teaching of Scripture to your life.

Who specifically is Jesus praying for (v. 20)? Why does this matter?

John 17 is often known as the "High Priestly Prayer." Jesus offered these words to His Father before He went to the cross. In this moment, Jesus chose to pray not only for His disciples there with Him but also for those who would believe in Him in the generations to come. He was praying for you and me, and He hasn't stopped (Heb. 7:25).

Jesus prays for us. Jesus followers pray for one another. Samuel said he wouldn't sin by failing to pray for the people of Israel (1 Sam. 12:23). Paul prayed for almost every church to whom he wrote in the New Testament. If Jesus followers are to be rightly related to one another, we must pray for one another.

Perhaps the greatest ministry you'll ever have in the lives of others is to consistently pray for them. Paul begged the churches in the New Testament to pray for him. There are some things God will do in the lives of others only if we pray. He has chosen to work that way. We need each other, and we desperately need to pray for one another. It's a great honor and privilege to lift the name of one another up to God in prayer. If you fail to pray for others, you're missing out on one of the greatest kingdom opportunities God has given you.

Do you take it seriously when someone asks you to pray for them? If not, what does that reflect about your feelings towards prayer?

Who is in your life that God may be asking you to pray for on a regular basis?

DAY 2
JESUS FOLLOWERS
ENCOURAGE ONE ANOTHER

READ

Read the following passages slowly and carefully.

> Matthew 14:22-27
>
> Acts 4:36
>
> Acts 9:26-27
>
> Acts 11:25-26
>
> Hebrews 10:24-25

INTERACT

Answer the following questions:

What does the Bible say?

What does the passage teach me about following Jesus?

REFLECT
Apply the teaching of Scripture to your life.

Everyone needs encouragement. Thankfully, God has designed it so that believers encourage one another. He desires that our walks with Him be personal but never private. One of the reasons He has given us each other is because we all need encouragement from one another in order to continue in the Christian life.

Scripture is filled with multiple examples of believers encouraging one another. This practice is rooted in the life of Jesus. He encouraged His weary disciples simply by His presence. Jesus continues to do that through the ministry of the Holy Spirit. In Acts 9, we see Barnabas ministering to Paul through encouragement. Barnabas gave him the necessary recommendation and support to earn the trust of those in Jerusalem.

Later in Acts 11, Barnabas traveled to Tarsus to look for Saul, later named Paul, who had evidently become discouraged in the ministry and gone home. The encouragement of Barnabas made an eternal difference in Paul's life. God knows every believer intimately and personally. He knows when we need encouragement and is kind enough to send it to us through the words, prayers, and presence of other believers.

1 Thessalonians 5:11 tells us to encourage one another and build one another up. Are there any corrections you need to make in light of this instruction from Scripture?

Who needs your encouragement right now? What is one small way you can encourage them today?

There are a myriad ways to encourage one another. Ask God to bring to mind or to put in your path today someone whome you can build up and encourage.

DAY 3
JESUS FOLLOWERS ARE MEMBERS OF ONE ANOTHER

READ

Read the following passages slowly and carefully.

> **Romans 12:1-5**
>
> **Ephesians 1:22-23**
>
> **Ephesians 4:14-16**
>
> **Ephesians 5:30**

INTERACT

Answer the following questions:

What does the Bible say?

What does the passage teach me about following Jesus?

REFLECT
Apply the teaching of Scripture to your life.

What does it mean that we're members of one another?

Romans 12 exhorts us to offer ourselves to God as holy and living sacrifices. In Christ, we present ourselves to Him daily as living, holy, and acceptable sacrifice for Him to use as He pleases. From there, Paul dicsussed how believers relate to one another in the body of Christ. We can offer ourselves to God by offering ourselves to one another.

It's impossible to be a Jesus follower and not rightly relate to His Body—the church. Every believer is connected to every other believer by virtue of the fact that we all make up one body—the body of Christ. This body has many parts. Not every part does has the same function, but all are important. The overall health of the entire body and each individual member is dependent upon each part functioning properly. Again, we're members of one another.

We see this most clearly in the local church. The Bible describes the church as a body with many members. Not all members have the same function, but all are important. What one member does affects every other member. Jesus grows His body, but He does so as the parts of the body help each other grow. Thus, the overall health of the Church is directly related to Jesus followers being connected in community with one another. The relationship between believers in the body of Christ has no parallel in the world. We're members of one another. Tomorrow we'll learn more about how we rightly relate to one another in the Body of Christ—the Church

Do you contribute to the overall health of your local church, or do you hinder it?

Are you willing to ask God to show you how you can specifically offer yourself as a living sacrifice in order to help the church grow?

DAY 4
JESUS FOLLOWERS
ARE MEMBERS OF
ONE ANOTHER PART 2

READ
Read the following passage slowly and carefully.

1 Corinthians 12:11-27

INTERACT
Answer the following questions:

What does the Bible say?

What does the passage teach me about following Jesus?

REFLECT
Apply the teaching of Scripture to your life.

In the space below, write the verse number in the blank that teaches the principle after it. You may have to read the passage several times. The first one is done for you.

VERSE(S)

__11__   *The Holy Spirit decides who has what gifts and responsibilities.*

_____   *Those members with less prominent roles deserve more honor.*

_____   *The body isn't complete without every member functioning properly.*

_____   *If every member had the same function, the body wouldn't be complete.*

_____   *We need each other.*

_____   *There are many members but one body.*

_____   *No member is less important than any other member.*

_____   *God adds to the body as He desires.*

_____   *If one member suffers, all suffer.*

_____   *The less prominent parts are absolutely necessary.*

_____   *There shouldn't be any division in the body.*

Jesus is concerned about and active in His church. He is the Head, and He is in charge. Our role and responsibility in the church is up to Him. He even adds to the body as He sees fit (v. 18). He has so designed it that no member can work in isolation from any other member. We need each other. The health of the Church is dependent upon us rightly relating to one another.

DAY 5
JESUS FOLLOWERS
ARE GIFTED TO SERVE
ONE ANOTHER

READ
Read the following passages slowly and carefully.

> **1 Corinthians 12:4-11**
>
> **1 Peter 4:10-11**
>
> **Romans 12:6**

INTERACT
Answer the following questions:

What does the Bible say?

What does the passage teach me about following Jesus?

REFLECT
Apply the teaching of Scripture to your life.

In 1 Peter 4, the word Peter uses for gift comes from the word that is often translated *grace* in the New Testament. This means that spiritual gifts are the result of God's grace in our lives. They're undeserved, gracious, divine gifts.

At the moment of salvation, every believer is uniquely gifted by the Holy Spirit to serve one another. Gifts are not a substance; they're a manifestation of a Person—the Spirit. Thus, only when we're in right relation to Him will we use our gifts properly. The Holy Spirit decides who has what gifts. To compare and covet the gifts of others is therefore to question the wisdom of God. Peter breaks down the gifts into serving and speaking. Both bring glory to God.

The Bible makes a few things clear about spiritual gifts. Every believer has at least one gift (1 Pet. 4:10), and no one has all the gifts (1 Cor. 7:7). The use of spiritual gifts without love is worthless (1 Cor. 13:1-3). When we're rightly following Jesus, we see the church not as a place that exists to meet our needs, but as a community where Christ in us can meet the needs of others through the gifts He has given each of us.

How has God gifted you to bring Him the most glory?

If you don't know how God has gifted you, who is a minister or church leader you could connect with about serving? When will you contact them?

If you don't use your spiritual gifts, what are you depriving the church of?

Spiritual gifts are best discovered by being an active part of your local church. Spiritual gift tests may help, but ultimately over time and through involvement you'll discover areas of service where you're most fulfilled and fruitful. You'll learn, and others will notice. Those are likely areas of gifting.

WEEK 6
SHARE
I HAVE A MISSION

Start

Welcome to week 6 of *The Life of a Jesus Follower*. This week and next we'll shift into talking about Christ's relationship with those who don't know God at all. To think about this relationship of Jesus we're going to use the word SHARE.

What was your biggest lesson from the CONNECT section of our study?

Who is the first person you remember sharing the gospel with you?

So far in our time together we've seen that following Jesus isn't about you living for Jesus, but actually about Jesus living His life through you. If Jesus really is living through us, our lives will look increasingly like His. And Jesus loved people who didn't know God.

Think about the woman at the well or the Roman centurion who approached Jesus for help—Jesus stopped and cared for these people thoughtfully, intentionally, and without hurry. The Gospels are filled with accounts of Jesus taking time to minister to people who didn't know God. If Jesus valued these relationships, we must as well.

Ask someone to pray, then watch the video teaching.

Watch

Use this section to take notes as you watch video session 6.

Discuss

Use the following questions to facilitate a conversation with your group.

Read Romans 10:14. What does this verse teach us about the necessity of Jesus followers telling other people about Jesus?

Vance said God's plan is the whole church taking the whole gospel to the whole world. Do you see this as your responsibility? Why or why not?

Read John 12:45-46. What does it mean for Jesus to be "light"? How does Jesus reveal who God is?

Read Matthew 5:14-16. How does Jesus living in us lead us to be lights in the world?

Read John 6:38. What did Jesus come to earth to do? If we're sent by Jesus what does it look like for us to do His will?

Read 2 Corinthians 2:14-17 for the remaining questions.

How might followers of Jesus be the "fragrance of Christ" (v. 14) to the world around us?

How is our desire to share Jesus with the world related to the work He is already doing in our lives?

Where are some places Jesus is or could be using you to spread His light?

Pause for a moment and pray together.
- *Pray for a growing desire to share God's love with the world.*
- *Ask God to show you places where you can share Jesus locally.*
- *Ask God to use you to bring His light to your friends who have yet to believe.*

After praying, remind the group to complete the five personal studies.

DAY 1
A JESUS FOLLOWER
KNOWS THE GOD
OF THE WORLD

READ
Read the following passage slowly and carefully.

Psalm 46:10

INTERACT
Answer the following questions:

What does the Bible say?

What does the passage teach me about following Jesus?

REFLECT
Apply the teaching of Scripture to your life.

This verse seems to be two separate thoughts in one verse:

"Be still, and know that I am God" and
"I will be exalted among the nations..."

Many people quote the first half of the verse without the second half, but they're related.

What does "being still" have to do with "knowing God"?

How does the first thought in the verse relate to the second?

One of the joys of being a Christian is spending time in silence and stillness with the Most High God. What God encourages in the Scriptures we often neglect—daily, deep devotion to Him. It's no accident that this psalm attributes quiet contemplation about who God is—"know that I am God"—with the remarkable realization of what He is doing—"being exalted among the nations."

As we grow closer to Him in communion and devotion each day, we look outward with Him to the harvest in the world. As we gain a heart for Him, He gives us His heart for the world. As we fall in love with the King, we'll want others to know and love as well. We'll begin to develop a love for the things He loves.

It's God's ultimate goal to be glorified among all the nations of the earth. In your time alone with God, do you ponder these things? Why or why not?

Does the fact that He wants us to "be still" mean we shouldn't be active in His work? Explain.

DAY 2
A JESUS FOLLOWER HAS A MISSION TO THE WORLD

READ
Read the following passages slowly and carefully.

Acts 1:8

John 20:21

2 Corinthians 5:17-20

INTERACT
Answer the following questions:

What does the Bible say?

What does the passage teach me about following Jesus?

REFLECT
Apply the teaching of Scripture to your life.

What is a witness?

What does it mean to be reconciled to someone? What does it mean for God to give us a ministry of reconciliation?

God has brought us into a relationship with Himself because He loves us, but the reality is that He has also brought us into relationship with Himself because He loves the people around us. The way He makes Himself known to those around us is through our witness, which means sharing our personal stories of knowing Jesus with those around us. Many people refer to Acts 1:8 by saying something like this: "We have got to reach our own 'Jerusalem,' then our 'Judea and Samaria,' and then the 'uttermost parts,'" as if we could not be a witness to the nations until we reach our hometowns. However, the verse actually says that we should do "both/and." Our mission is both local and global. Every believer is called to simultaneously have a mission both locally and globally. While the particular role each of us fills may be different, the responsibility to be a witness through sharing our story both locally and globally remains.

In 2 Corinthians 5, Paul refers to us as "ambassadors." What does an ambassador do? Reflect on the ways God has made you an ambassador for Christ where you live, where you work, and where you play.

DAY 3
A JESUS FOLLOWER
HAS A HEART
FOR THE WORLD

READ

Read the following passages slowly and carefully.

> Romans 10:12-15
>
> Matthew 28: 18-20

INTERACT

Answer the following questions:

What does the Bible say?

What does the passage teach me about following Jesus?

REFLECT
Apply the teaching of Scripture to your life.

Is having a heart for the world optional for Jesus followers? Why or why not?

Billions of people around the world have little to no access to the gospel. The Bible makes it clear that someone must go and tell them. That's why God left us here as opposed to drawing us up to heaven at the moment of our salvation.

There are roughly 12,000 people groups in the world today. A people group is a distinctive group of people with their own culture, language, and identity. The biblical word for these groups is "nation." It's not necessarily defined by a country's boundary or nationality. Political borders are man-made, but people groups are made by God. Of these 12,000 people groups, more than 3,000 of them haven't yet been reached with the gospel. These unreached people groups have very little, if any, Christian witness among them.

We often divide people in the world into two groups—the saved and the lost. But that simply measures the response to the gospel. Let's think of the world a different way—those who have heard the gospel and those who haven't. This measures the accessibility of the gospel. When we think of the people of the world this way, we have to face the fact that nearly one-third of the world still has no access to the gospel!

Matthew 28:18-20 is a command and not a suggestion. Jesus commanded us to make disciples of all nations (people groups). God desires to use our jobs, skills, and passions to engage in His mission of taking the gospel to every people group on planet earth.

How can you use your job, skill, or passion to accomplish the mission?

It's clear that the nations who have yet to hear the gospel are on God's heart. What are you doing to take the gospel to the nations?

DAY 4
A JESUS FOLLOWER
JOINS GOD'S ACTIVITY

READ

Read the following passages slowly and carefully.

> John 3:16
>
> John 4:35; 5:17
>
> Matthew 9:37-38

INTERACT

Answer the following questions:

What does the Bible say?

What does the passage teach me about following Jesus?

REFLECT
Apply the teaching of Scripture to your life.

God's work is happening all around us whether we know it or not. Our work as followers of Jesus is to join in God's work when we recognize it around us. Jesus saw the Father working, and He only did what the Father told Him to do. How often do we jump ahead of God and do things we think are "good works" only to find out later that God never really intended for us to do those things? God is definitely working in the world. There is great evidence of His activity throughout history and all around us today. The question is, are we watching for His activity around us?

But how do we discover and enter into this work? We pray, asking God by His Spirit, to give us eyes to see His work around us. Then we look for His activity in the lives of people in our families, workplaces, schools, and neighborhoods. God wants us to share in His mission where you live, work, and play. Using our jobs, skills, or passions, God invites us to join in His activity around us in our neighborhoods and among the nations.

Who in your circle of influence can you sense God working among?
How might God use you to join in His activity in this person's life?

Where do you see God at work in your city? How might God use your job,
skill, or passion to engage in His activity in your city?

Take a moment and pray that God will reveal His work around you.

DAY 5
A JESUS FOLLOWER
PRAYS FOR THE WORLD

READ
Read the following passages slowly and carefully.

> James 5:16
>
> Ephesians 2:18
>
> Ephesians 3:11-12

INTERACT
Answer the following questions:

What does the Bible say?

What does the passage teach me about following Jesus?

REFLECT
Apply the teaching of Scripture to your life.

One of the ways we join in God's activity in the world is through prayer. When James says the prayers of the righteous are effective, it doesn't mean that God is more inclined to answer their prayers but that their prayers are already more in line with God's will because the righteous have a desire to be close to the heart of God.

Additionally, God in His sovereignty has chosen to limit His activity to the prayers of His people. There's a lot about that reality that we simply don't understand, but it doesn't change the fact that it's true, according to God's Word. In His wisdom, God uses the prayers of weak and finite people to play a part in the unfolding of His sovereign will.

While it's true that God doesn't need us (or anything) to accomplish His will, God has chosen to work through us as we pray. What might God do through us if we chose to seek Him desperately in prayer?

Think about the kinds of prayers that, when answered, would change entire people groups forever. Think about a prayer that, when answered, would change you forever. Often we see God working in limited ways because we offer limited prayers. The throne of grace is open to us. Let us be bold in our prayers.

Who can you pray for who doesn't know Jesus?

If God answered all your prayers, what difference would it make in your life?

What difference would it make in the world?

How might your prayers need to change as a result of what you've learned this week?

WEEK 7
SHARE
THE MISSION IS BIG

Start

Welcome to week 7 of *The Life of a Jesus Follower*. This week we'll continue to talk about what it means to SHARE in Jesus' mission to the world.

> *How did the last session and personal studies cause you to shift your understanding of our mission to the world?*

> *What's a hobby or interest you would say you're passionate about?*

We give time to what we're passionate about. If you're a sports fan, you likely make time to watch games. You own the gear. You know the starting line-ups. If you care about your yard, you make sure it's cut, watered, and fertilized. You'll keep the flowerbeds weeded and the bushes trimmed. No matter what it is, all passions take time and intentionality.

Throughout this study, we've seen that if we're going to follow Jesus, His life must be lived through our lives. If that's true, we must be passionate about what Jesus is passionate about. We must give our time to what Jesus prioritizes. If we look through the Gospels, it becomes clear that Jesus was passionate about expanding the kingdom of God so that all people could know the saving power of the Father. We'll think about that passion together in this session.

Ask someone to pray, then watch the video teaching.

Watch

Use this section to take notes as you watch video session 7.

Discuss

Use the following questions to facilitate a conversation with your group.

Read Luke 4:42-43.

How closely does your heart reflect Jesus' in these verses? How often do you feel like you must be about God's work in the world?

How have we made missions another church program instead of the passion of Jesus' life?

How does making missions a program of the church make the calling to be a witness seem optional?

Read Matthew 6:33. What is the kingdom, and what does it look like to see it first in our lives? Who do you know that models this well?

Read Matthew 24:14. How does the expanse of the kingdom of God tie to our mission to the nations?

Vance said one of the greatest tools of the devil is the self-centeredness of God's people. How does being self-centered rob our passion for mission?

Where have you prioritized your own kingdom above Jesus'?

The church shares in the mission of Jesus together. What are a few ways we can encourage one another to be involved in God's mission locally and globally?

Pause for a moment and pray together.
- *Ask for renewed passion for God's work in the world.*
- *Request courage to be a witness when and where God calls you to be one.*
- *Pray for opportunities to share the love of Christ with the world.*

After praying, remind the group to complete the five personal studies.

DAY 1
A JESUS FOLLOWER
INVESTS IN GOD'S ACTIVITY

READ
Read the following passages slowly and carefully.

> Philippians 1:3-5
>
> Philippians 4:15-20

INTERACT
Answer the following questions:

What does the Bible say?

What does the passage teach me about following Jesus?

REFLECT
Apply the teaching of Scripture to your life.

Since the beginning of the movement that you and I know as following Jesus, radical generosity has always been a common expression of the gospel through the church. God's plan has always been to provide for His mission through His people.

Philippians shows us an example of one church that saw giving as an opportunity to join in God's activity in the world. God is at work all around us. One way He invites us to join in what He is doing is through generosity. Jesus followers have always regularly given a portion of what God has given to them as an investment in His mission. And at times—as we see in Philippians—Jesus followers have given in ways that involved extreme sacrifice. We don't give in order to be good Christians. We give with hearts of joy, in response to God's greatness, and out of the overflow of the impact of His glorious gospel in our lives. We don't give to a church but through a church as an investment in God's activity locally and globally. We're never more like Jesus than when we give. The gospel at its core is a message of generosity. John 3:16 states that God so loved the world that He gave. As Christ begins to live His life through us, one expression of that is radical generosity. Part of living generously as an investment in God's activity is establishing the right target for our lives when it comes to stewarding God's resources.

> *Can I honestly say I live generously, investing in God's activity in the world? If not, what needs to change?*

> *Do I give regularly, proportionately, and sometimes sacrificially to join in God's kingdom work?*

DAY 2
A JESUS FOLLOWER
LIVES SENT

READ
Read the following passages slowly and carefully.

John 17:3-21

John 20:21

INTERACT
Answer the following questions:

What does the Bible say?

What does the passage teach me about following Jesus?

REFLECT
Apply the teaching of Scripture to your life.

The longest conversation recorded in Scripture between God the Father and God the Son is found in John 17. This powerful chapter provides a glimpse of the intimate relationship between Jesus and the Father and allows us insight to the moments just before Jesus is arrested, beaten, and crucified.

In a significant and precious moment, Jesus spent time praying for His Church. You'll notice, in praying for His Church, Jesus didn't pray for buildings, worship services, an address, or an event. Jesus prayed for people, His people—the Church! The Church Jesus established was and is a community of people who have been called and then sent out to share in His mission. Jesus said, "As You sent Me into the world, I also have sent them." The word "sent" indicates deployment with a purpose. The reality is that the people of God have been deployed as missionaries into the world. That means as a Jesus follower, God has sent you as a missionary.

God passionately loves the peoples of the earth, and He desires for them to be transformed by the gospel. He has sent His people, the Church, into the world as missionaries to leverage their influence for the sake of His kingdom. God has strategically placed us as His missionaries in workplaces, neighborhoods, schools, and cities in order for our lives to demonstrate His life to the world.

How can you leverage your influence for the sake of His kingdom?

What often hinders you from living sent as a missionary where God has placed you (e.g. fear, busyness, etc.)?

Take a moment and surrender your hindrances to God in prayer.

DAY 3
A JESUS FOLLOWER
MAKES DISCIPLES
ALL OVER THE WORLD

READ
Read the following passages slowly and carefully.

> 2 Timothy 2:2
>
> 1 Thessalonians 2:1-12
>
> Mark 3:14
>
> Matthew 28:18-20

INTERACT
Answer the following questions:

What does the Bible say?

What does the passage teach me about following Jesus?

REFLECT
Apply the teaching of Scripture to your life.

Based on the previous Scriptures, in your own words answer the following questions:

What is discipleship?

What is the activity of discipleship?

Jesus said to His followers in Matthew 28, "make disciples." He had modeled it to them for three and a half years. He had poured His life into a group of twelve men and was now calling them to do the same. All Jesus followers can make disciples. All Jesus followers may not go about it in the same way, but all can do it.

Discipleship is investing into the life of another so that the life of Jesus may be reproduced in them. It's more than teaching. It's more than a class. It involves your life.
Making disciples involves sharing the truth. Paul told Timothy to "teach what he had learned." Thus, making disciples demands that you must be continually growing yourself. Making disciples involves time. Paul said that he imparted to the Thessalonians his very life. Making disciples involves work.

Paul modeled this lifestyle of discipleship. Making disciples is like being a father. Where mothers are generally more nurturing, fathers challenge us to move ahead with encouragement and discipline. The ultimate goal is Christ-likeness. The life of Jesus is lived out in individual Jesus followers who then impact and invest in the lives of other Jesus followers.

What needs to change in your own life to give more time and energy to the cause of making disciples?

DAY 4
A JESUS FOLLOWER
WILL FACE OPPOSITION

READ

Read the following passages slowly and carefully.

Matthew 5:10-12,44

John 15:18-25

Acts 5:41

Romans 12:17-21

1 Peter 2:23

1 Peter 4:12-16

INTERACT

Answer the following questions:

What does the Bible say?

What does the passage teach me about following Jesus?

REFLECT
Apply the teaching of Scripture to your life.

According to these verses, what is to be our attitude if we suffer or face difficulty as Christians? How are we to respond to God and those who oppose us?

Expect opposition. Following Jesus isn't consistent with the direction the rest of the world is going. Though we may not face death because we're Christians, there will be opposition if we follow Christ in this fallen world. Jesus said it would happen. The world nailed Him to a cross.

Matthew 5 says we're blessed if we suffer for the sake of righteousness. If you miss out on something or are overlooked by someone because you follow Jesus, you're blessed. Jesus says, "rejoice," your reward will be great. The early disciples rejoiced when they were considered worthy to suffer for His name (Acts 5:41).

Peter said not to be surprised at difficulty as though something strange was happening. He said the Spirit of glory and God rests on those who suffer. He goes on to say that suffering as an evildoer or as one who does wrong isn't pleasing to God. The suffering referred to is due to godly living in a godless world, not for wrongdoing.

When others hurt you, laugh at you, leave you out, or pass you over because you're a Christian, the Bible gives you actions to take. You must first respond to God. Trust Him to carry out vengeance and to give you peace. God will take care of you and the situation. Second, we're to pray for our persecutors and do good to them. In that way, you give a powerful testimony to the power of God in your life. This will not come naturally but only as you're led and empowered by the Spirit of Christ.

What's your response when being a Jesus follower costs you something? Do you rejoice? Do you trust His promises? If not, why not?

How do you respond to those who hurt you? Who might you need to pray for in light of these verses?

DAY 5
A JESUS FOLLOWER
PRIORITIZES THE KINGDOM

READ
Read the following passages slowly and carefully.

> Matthew 24:14
>
> Revelation 5:9-10
>
> Revelation 11:15
>
> Luke 12:31-32

INTERACT

Answer the following questions:
What does the Bible say?

What does the passage teach me about following Jesus?

REFLECT
Apply the teaching of Scripture to your life.

There are more than 100 references in 16 books of the New Testament to the kingdom of God. And yet the kingdom of God is a concept that the church often misunderstands. The kingdom of God is God's sovereign activity resulting in people being in right relationship with Him. To say it another way, the kingdom of God is the big picture of God's activity all over the world. Here are three realities about the kingdom that will help us understand it practically.

1. The kingdom is believers (Rev. 5:9-10). The kingdom is made up of all the followers of Jesus all over the world.
2. The kingdom is big (Rev. 5:9). It contains believers from every tribe, tongue, people, and nation. The kingdom of God is bigger than any church, denomination, city, or nation.
3. The kingdom is being built (Matt. 24:14). As you read this, God is alive and at work all over the world building His kingdom. We're living in exciting days to be part of God's global harvest.

The way God is expanding His Kingdom is through His church. The local church is the gathering place to teach people about the King and to disciple them in kingdom living. The local church is also the launching pad for the expansion of God's kingdom locally and globally. As followers of Jesus we've all been invited to join in God's activity. We're not simply members of a church; we're citizens of a kingdom that is alive and expanding all over the world.

How can you prioritize the kingdom in your life?

What is one change you'll make based on your time in the Scriptures this week?

WEEK 8
UNBURDENED

Start

Welcome to week 8 of *The Life of a Jesus Follower*. Thanks for sticking through this study. Hopefully, this time has been helpful as we've studied the three relationships Jesus lived in. This week, we're going to look at how to put those relationships into practice in our own lives.

What is your biggest takeaway from the SHARE portion of the study?

What's a relationship in your life you've seen grow as you've intentionally devoted time to that relationship ?

All relationships grow in direct proportion to the amount of time we invest in them. Our relationship with Jesus is no different. Through this study, we've seen that being a Jesus follower is all about relationships. We've taken a deep dive into the three relationships Jesus walked in—His relationship with the Father, His relationships with the disciples, and His relationship with people who didn't know God at all.

As Jesus followers, the desire of our hearts should be to look like Jesus. In this last week of our study, we're going to see how the rhythms of our lives can intentionally mirror the rhythms of Jesus' life. When we give time to ABIDE in Christ personally and daily, CONNECT in large group and small groups, and SHARE locally and globally, the life of Jesus will begin to pour out of us as He begins to live in and through us.

Ask someone to pray, then watch the video teaching.

Watch

Use this section to take notes as you watch video session 8.

Discuss

Use the following questions to facilitate a conversation with your group.

Read Mark 1:35. There's no substitute for time spent alone with God. If you've developed a regular Bible study habit, share what your time with God looks like. How has it grown your relationship with Jesus?

How does spending regular time alone with God impact our relationships with other people? Give a few examples.

Read Luke 4:16 and Hebrews 10:24-25. Why is it essential that we gather together with other believers? What do you gain from this time each week?

What does spending time in a discipleship group like this one give us things we can't get elsewhere?

Read Luke 19:10 and Acts 1:8. How do we see the mission of the Father in the life of Jesus?

Where are some key partnerships we can serve with locally? What would it look like for us to serve together as a group? Where might God be leading you to serve globally?

Would you be willing to take the five percent challenge? Who will hold you accountable?

What's your biggest takeaway from our eight sessions together?

Pause for a moment and pray together.
- *Ask God to take what you've learned in this study and lead you into a deeper relationship with Him.*
- *Pray that you would continue to commit your life to the same three relationships Jesus committed His life to.*
- *Pray that the world would be changed as Jesus' life and light begins to be lived through you.*

After praying, remind the group to complete the five personal studies.

DAY 1
A JESUS FOLLOWER
SPENDS TIME WITH GOD

READ
Read the following passages slowly and carefully.

Mark 1:35

2 Timothy 3:16-17

Psalm 119:103-105

INTERACT
Answer the following questions:

What does the Bible say?

What does the passage teach me about following Jesus?

REFLECT
Apply the teaching of Scripture to your life.

How do these passages describe the Bible?

Hopefully, through this study, you've seen the benefits of investing in the same relationships Jesus Himself invested in. Over the next five days, we're going to focus on *how* to invest in these relationships.

The first investment is "God Time." This is time spent daily alone in fellowship with God. Jesus modeled this for us by giving priority time in His own life to being alone with the Father. In the same way, it's imperative that you choose daily to set aside time to be alone with Jesus. Everything in your life will rise and fall based on your time alone with Him.

For us, this means we devote one percent of our day (around 15 minutes) to Bible study and prayer. If you've been working through the personal studies each week, you're well on your way to establishing this habit. When we come to the words of Scripture, we're reading God's own words. That's what Paul meant when he said the Scriptures were "God-breathed" or "inspired" (2 Tim. 3:16).

Through the inspiration of the Spirit of God, the Bible is written in such a way that though the human authors are willing and integral participants, the very words of Scripture are God's own words. To spend time reading the Bible is to spend time hearing directly from God.

Additionally, through prayer, we have the ability to commune with God—to speak to Him and hear back from Him. When you devote one percent of your day to spending time with God, that will impact the remaining 99 percent of your day. So find a time and place, and meet with God daily.

When and where will you spend time alone with God?

How will you guard this time so that other things don't over take this priority?

DAY 2
A JESUS FOLLOWER
GATHERS IN WORSHIP

READ

Read the following passages slowly and carefully.

> Hebrews 10:24-25
>
> Psalm 95:1-3
>
> Acts 2:46

INTERACT

Answer the following questions:

What does the Bible say?

What does the passage teach me about following Jesus?

REFLECT
Apply the teaching of Scripture to your life.

The second strategic way you must choose to invest your life is in"Gather Time." Today we'll focus on the one percent of your week (or about an hour and a half) as a Jesus follower that you spend worshiping with your church family. The regular worship time at your local church might be more or less than an hour and a half. The point here is that you agree to prioritize gathering in worship with your church.

In Scripture, church worship isn't merely suggested; it's commanded. We live in a day where a "regular" church attendee is someone who comes once a month, but the Bible calls us to a much higher standard. Again, we see this modeled in the life of Christ. Before His death, burial, and resurrection, it was Jesus' custom to gather in the synagogue with God's people on the Sabbath day for worship. And this Sabbath practice of Jesus became the Sunday pattern of the early church after the resurrection. This is an essential part of following Jesus, not something we commit to when our travel schedule and kid's ball games permit.

When we gather for worship, we're not simply following some American version of Christianity. We're following in the footsteps of Jesus and the early church in prioritizing the public worship of God together with God's family.

> *Would you say you prioritize worshipping at your local church? If not, what priorities are you allowing to keep you from church?*

> *What adjustments can you make to your schedule to ensure you're committed to gathering with God's people?*

> *What blessings have you received by meeting with God and His people in worship?*

DAY 3
A JESUS FOLLOWER
GATHERS IN SMALL GROUPS

READ
Read the following passages slowly and carefully.

> Colossians 3:12-17
>
> Mark 3:14-15
>
> Acts 2:42-47
>
> Romans 12:9-19

INTERACT
Answer the following questions:

What does the Bible say?

What does the passage teach me about following Jesus?

REFLECT
Apply the teaching of Scripture to your life.

Based on these passages, how does God expect Christians to live with one another?

How closely does your community mirror the community described in the New Testament?

The next way Jesus followers should invest their time is in "Group Time"—that means devoting one percent of your month (or about seven hours) in community with people you care about and who care about you. That's seven hours of doing life together.

This might look like a traditional Sunday School class. It may mean meeting with a smaller group of men or women. It might look like a group meeting in a home. Maybe it's the group of people you're working through this study with. The exact expression is less important than the intent. God has designed our lives as Jesus followers to happen in the context of community.

Throughout the New Testament, community is assumed. Jesus sought it with His disciples. Luke describes the early Christian community in the book of Acts. The New Testament letters were written to communities of faith across the known world. Revelation culminates in the community of God worshiping Him at His throne. The New Testament is all about Christian community, so you shouldn't live without it. Whether you've found that community already or are still searching, find a group of Jesus followers, connect to them, and commit to them. There is no substitute for Christian community anywhere else in the world.

When will you meet with brothers and sisters in Christ for group time?
If you're already doing this, how has it impacted your faith in Jesus?

DAY 4
A JESUS FOLLOWER SHARES LOCALLY AND GLOBALLY

READ

Read the following passages slowly and carefully.

> Acts 1:8
>
> Mathew 5:14-16
>
> Mathew 28:19-20

INTERACT

Answer the following questions:

What does the Bible say?

What does the passage teach me about following Jesus?

REFLECT
Apply the teaching of Scripture to your life.

The final way you must choose to invest your time to grow as a follower of Jesus is in "Go Time." This is time spent going on mission with God locally and globally. This was the most obvious time modeled by Jesus. His entire life was spent on mission with God. You can begin to share in God's mission right where you are, but you can't fulfill your responsibility to fully engage in God's mission without being intentional to tell the good news of Jesus globally.

Practically speaking, this means spending two percent of your year invested in "Go Time." That means approximately seven days each year when you intentionally share in God's mission through serving opportunities, going on trips, and leveraging your job, skills, and passions locally and/or globally.

As the life of Jesus is lived through us before other people, His light begins to bear on the world and beat back the darkness. As we saw earlier in this study, our mission to the world is big. Here are a couple of simple ways to connect to God's mission in the world.

First, begin to pray about what's breaking your heart in the world. Is it poverty? Fatherlessness? An unreached people group? These heartaches might be the means God is using to call you into His mission. Pray and ask for wisdom for where to get involved.

Next, reach out to a church leader and find out what existing partnerships your church has in your community and around the world. Consider the opportunities before you, and prayerfully consider where God would have you share His light in the world.

Is there anywhere you would like to get plugged into sharing Christ's light in the world? What steps will you take this week?

Who might you enlist to serve with you?

DAY 5
A JESUS FOLLOWER
LIVES UNBURDENED

READ
Read the following passages slowly and carefully.

Matthew 11:28-30

2 Corinthians 11:3

INTERACT
Answer the following questions:

What does the Bible say?

What does the passage teach me about following Jesus?

REFLECT
Apply the teaching of Scripture to your life.

At the outset of this study, Vance shared that the verses we read today didn't make sense to him. Maybe they didn't make sense to you either. Hopefully, at the end of this journey you've been able to embrace the truth that following Jesus is all about relationships. That's the whole point of this last week.

What we're calling the "Five Percent Life" is simply a starting point. It's not the target. The target is to faithfully follow Jesus as defined by the three relationships we've identified with God, one another, and the world. Following these steps doesn't earn you favor before God. They're guidelines to help you, not burdens to weigh you down. The Five Percent Life isn't a list to check off but a walkway to help you journey in relationship with Jesus.

Following Jesus should not be a burden. It's meant to be comforting and life-giving. If you embrace the Five Percent Life as a starting point, the other 95 percent of your life will be changed forever as you abide in Christ, connect in community, and share in the mission of God's kingdom.

The ultimate goal is that as you invest and walk in the same relationships that Jesus did. You'll be unburdened as you capture the simplicity of living the life of a Jesus follower.

What have you learned over the last eight sessions about following Jesus?

How do you expect your life to be different as a result of the time you've spent in this study?

Who needs to know what you've learned? When will you share with them?

TIPS FOR LEADING A SMALL GROUP

Prayerfully Prepare

Prepare for each group session with prayer. Ask the Holy Spirit to work through you and the group discussion as you point to Jesus each week through God's Word.

REVIEW the personal studies and the group sessions ahead of time.

PRAY for each person in the group.

Minimize Distractions

Do everything in your ability to help people focus on what's most important: connecting with God, with the Bible, and with one another.

Create a comfortable environment. If group members are uncomfortable, they'll be distracted and, therefore, not engaged in the group experience.

Take into consideration seating, temperature, lighting, refreshments, surrounding noise, and general cleanliness.

At best, thoughtfulness and hospitality show guests and group members they're welcome and valued in whatever environment you choose to gather. At worst, people may never notice your effort, but they're also not distracted.

Include Others

Your goal is to foster a community in which people are welcome just as they're, but are encouraged to grow spiritually. Always be aware of opportunities to include anyone who visits the group and invite new people to join your group.

Encourage Discussion

A good small-group experience has the following characteristics.

EVERYONE PARTICIPATES. Encourage everyone to ask questions, share responses, or read aloud.

NO ONE DOMINATES—NOT EVEN THE LEADER. Be sure your time speaking as a leader takes up less than half your time together as a group. Politely guide the discussion if anyone dominates.

NOBODY IS RUSHED THROUGH QUESTIONS. Don't feel that a moment of silence is a bad thing. People often need time to think about their responses to questions they've just heard or to gain courage to share what God is stirring in their hearts.

INPUT IS AFFIRMED AND FOLLOWED UP. Make sure you point out something true or helpful in a response. Don't just move on. Build community with follow-up questions, asking how other people have experienced similar things or how a truth has shaped their understanding of God and the Scripture you're studying. People are less likely to speak up if they fear that you don't actually want to hear their answers or that you're looking for only a certain answer.

GOD AND HIS WORD ARE CENTRAL. Opinions and experiences can be helpful, but God has given us the truth. Trust Scripture to be the authority and God's Spirit to work in people's lives. You can't change anyone, but God can. Continually point people to the Word and to active steps of faith.

Keep Connecting

Think of ways to connect with group members during the week. Participation during the group session always improves when members spend time connecting with one another outside the group sessions. The more people are comfortable with and involved in one another's lives, the more they'll look forward to being together. When people move beyond being friendly to truly being friends who form a community, they come to each session eager to engage instead of merely attending.

LEADER GUIDE

How to Use This Leader Guide

Prepare to Lead

Each session in the leader guide is designed to be cut out so that you, the leader, can keep this front-and-back page with you as you lead the group session.

Work through the personal studies, watch the session's teaching video, and read the group session with the leader guide cutout in hand to understand how it supplements each section of the group study.

Big Idea

This short statement captures the essence of the session.

Key Scriptures

Key passages of Scripture are listed for quick reference.

Conversation Helps

This section contains brief statements that summarize Vance's teaching. Use this section along with the questions in the "Discuss" section to guide help you facilitate the conversation in your group.

Considerations

This brief section contains a few thoughts about how to accommodate different kinds of people in your group.

SESSION 1

BIG IDEA

Following Jesus is all about relationships

KEY SCRIPTURES

2 Corinthians 11:3

John 15:5

John 15:12

John 17:18

John 13:34-35

CONVERSATION HELPS

This whole study has been designed to help us enter into and walk in the same three relationships that Jesus embraced.

Following Jesus means walking in the same relationships Jesus walked in

1. A love relationship with the Father
   - We ABIDE in Christ personally and daily.
2. In fellowship with our brothers and sisters in Christ
   - We CONNECT in community through large and small groups.
3. In relationships with the world—those who don't know God.
   - We SHARE in the mission locally and globally.

   - In our Christian journey, we gravitate towards doing and knowing because those things feel attainable to us.
   - In our Christian life, pursuing activity and knowledge only leaves us weary and exhausted.
   - Truly following Jesus is about entering into a relationship with Him.
   - This is freeing because real relationships aren't defined by what we do for someone or know about them—it certainly includes those things—but the essence of a

relationship is intimacy. Jesus lived in relationships with the Father, with His disciples, and with those who didn't know God.

- As we see God at work in the world, it will deepen our love for Him and our commitment to the church.
- All three relationships are interdependent and interrelated. As we begin to walk in the relationships Jesus walked in, His life will naturally flow out of us as He lives in and through us.

CONSIDERATIONS

There are likely people in your group who have believed the lie that following Jesus is about what you do for Jesus or what you know about Jesus—maybe you're one of them. The goal of this session isn't to make these folks feel bad but to help them find the freedom that comes from knowing Jesus through a relationship.

NOTES

_____

_____

_____

_____

_____

_____

_____

_____

_____

_____

_____

_____

_____

_____

BIG IDEA

Following Jesus is an invitation to pursue a relationship with God.

KEY SCRIPTURES

Mark 3:13-14

John 17:3

CONVERSATION HELPS

- Jesus doesn't choose disciples by accident.
- He didn't haphazardly invite the first people he came across. Luke 6:12-19 tells us that Jesus devoted time to prayer before He summoned the disciples to Himself.
- The word "summoned" means to call or to invite. Jesus extends all His disciples a personal invitation to enjoy a relationship with God.
- Jesus invited the disciples because He *loved them*. Jesus calls us to "be with Him."
- God wants to be in a relationship with you *more than* you want to be in a relationship with Him. All you need to do is accept the invitation Jesus offers.
- Once you accept the invitation, the primary calling on your life isn't to do something for Jesus. The primary call on your life is to be with Jesus.
- The overall goal of your whole life becomes to know God.
- Your daily goal is simply to spend time with Him.
- As you spend time with God, you grow in intimacy with Him, and that growing intimacy with the Father spills out into every other area of life.
- However, we allow numerous barriers—schedules, appointments, apathy, laziness, busyness, or other excuses—to keep us from spending time with God.
- If spending time with God is the daily goal of our lives, we must make time for it.

CONSIDERATIONS

Be aware that some in your group may have never developed any kind of devotional life. Here are a few suggestions for spending time alone with God, daily.

- Start by carving out fifteen minutes of uninterrupted time to be alone with God.
- Start in one of the Gospels—Matthew, Mark, Luke, or John—and read one chapter a day.
- Jot down few reflections about what you read using the following questions:
- What does this teach me about God?
- What does this teach me about sinful people?
- What does this teach me about Jesus?
- What does this teach me about how I should live?
- Pray that God would make His Word effective in your life.
- Don't beat yourself up if you miss a day.

NOTES

_____

_____

_____

_____

_____

_____

_____

_____

_____

_____

_____

_____

BIG IDEA

The primary call on our lives isn't to do something for Jesus but to be with Jesus. However, we don't spend time with Jesus because we allow our pride and self-sufficiency get in the way.

KEY SCRIPTURES

Matthew 11:28-30

John 8:32

Romans 6:6-7

1 Corinthians 10:13

James 4:6

John 14:21,23,31

CONVERSATIONS HELPS

This session is all about three questions that help us understand why we don't spend time with God.

- Does a Christian have to sin? No.
- Does a Christian want to sin? No.
- If we don't want to sin and we don't have to sin, why do we?

That answer is a little more complicated.

- We sin because we don't love God (John 14:15). We don't love God because we don't know God. We don't know God because we don't spend time with Him.
- We don't spend time with Him because we're prideful and self-sufficient people.
- James 4:6 says. "But He gives a greater grace. Therefore it says, 'God is opposed to the proud, but gives grace to the humble.'"
- We need to be people who humbly depended on God's grace.
- As we cultivate humility, we'll run to God freely in need. When we do this, according to John 14:23, God will disclose himself to us.
- When we come to Jesus in humility, we'll be eager to spend time with Him, which grows our love for Him and decreases our desire to sin.

CONSIDERATIONS

The questions in this section of the study are difficult and convicting. There may be more silence than you're used to as people take time to process what they've heard. Give them time. Don't feel like you have to fill every silence.

As much as you can, help people see that when Vance is advocating that we spend time with God, this isn't spending time with God simply in order to check a box. It's spending time with God by His grace and in order to know Him. The behavior looks the same, but the heart behind it's completely different.

At the end, challenge the group to consider the most impactful truths of the ABIDE section. This will be the first question in the start section next week.

NOTES

_____

_____

_____

_____

_____

_____

_____

_____

_____

_____

_____

_____

_____

_____

_____

_____

BIG IDEA

*God created us to enjoy a relationship with Him
in the context of relationships with others.*

KEY SCRIPTURES

Genesis 1:26; 2:18

Acts 2:41

John 1:12

Romans 8:15-16

1 John 4:20-21

Matthew 5:23-25

CONVERSATION HELPS

- Our faith in Jesus is deeply personal, but it was never meant to be private. From the very beginning, God meant us to live out our faith in the context of a community.
- God Himself has eternally existed in the community of the Trinity—Father, Son, and Spirit.
- Our innate desire for community is one of the ways we know we've been made in God's image.
- The entirety of the Bible was written to a group of people: first, the nation of Israel, then to the church of Jesus Christ. All of the New Testament letters were written to churches throughout the known world.
- The church isn't a place or an event but God's collected people. We're a family who relates to one another as brothers and sisters with God as their Father.
- The relationships that exist inside the church will exist forever because we'll still be connected to other Christians in eternity.
- Christian community reflects the goodness of God. As our relationship with Him grows our desire to connect with other Christians will also grow.

CONSIDERATIONS

Are there people in your gathering who come to a group study but don't regularly attend a worship service at church? If so, you'll want to anticipate that tension and gently help them see why both are beneficial and needed to build their faith.

Many in your group likely think of church as an event to attended or a building with a physical address. One of the aims of this session is to correct that misunderstanding.

This would be a good week to find a way to connect with the members of this group outside of the traditional group meeting time if you aren't already spending time together outside of the group.

Lastly, there might be people in your group who carry wounds from a previous experience with Christian community. Keep this in mind, and be attentive and sincere if someone expresses a concern while pointing them back to God's plan for community in the Bible.

NOTES

_____

_____

_____

_____

_____

_____

_____

_____

_____

_____

_____

_____

_____

BIG IDEA

At the core of Christianity is the principle that we're to live out our relationship with God in fellowship with other believers.

KEY SCRIPTURES

Acts 2:42-47

Proverbs 27:17

1 John 4:12

CONVERSATION HELPS

Three cornerstone truths guide this conversation.

First, we need others to grow in intimacy with God.

- The early church devoted themselves to God and one another. These relationships weren't isolated but interdependent.
- Their relationships with one another positively impacted their relationship with God.
- The New Testament contains more than forty "one another" commands that we can't obeyed outside of the context of Christian community.

Second, we need others to walk through the ups and downs of life.

- God gave you other people as a gift. To reject Christian community is to spurn this gift.
- The early church jumped to action as needs arose. The early church was a community without need because each member played a part in serving one another.
- God cares so much about this community that He gave each of us gifts to care for and support one another.

Finally, we need each other to accomplish the mission.

- The "you" in the Great Commission is plural. Our mission to the world is truly *our* mission.
- One of the reasons people flocked to the early church was the early Christians' obvious commitment to one another.

CONSIDERATIONS

If people in this group are new to the life of the church, help them to see that church isn't a series of events but a real family. Fellowship can't happen if we only see each other once a week. Our relationships with other believers must be real and vital friendships that extend beyond the boundaries of regular church meetings like a worship services or small group meetings.

If time allows, figure out how you can best support one another and fulfill the commands of Christ. What specific needs exist in the group? How can we meet them together? Thinking through questions like this will help your group know that your commitment to Christian community is real and not just something limited to this group meeting.

Lastly, if the members of your group are members of your church, try and gauge whether or not they're involved and using their spiritual gifts. If not, help them get connected to a church leader that can get them plugged in, so they're equipped for service.

NOTES

_____

_____

_____

_____

_____

_____

_____

_____

_____

_____

_____

_____

_____

_____

_____

_____

BIG IDEA

God's plan is for the whole church to bring the whole gospel to the whole world.

KEY SCRIPTURES

Romans 10:14

John 6:38

John 12:45-46

John 17:18

Matthew 5:14

2 Corinthians 2:14-17

CONVERSATION HELPS

- The world is filled with 7.7 billion people made in the image of God. Among that number are billions of people made in God's image who don't know and aren't following Jesus.
- Scripture teaches that each of us is called to take the gospel of Jesus Christ to these billions of people.
- Jesus was sent to seek and save the lost (Luke 19:10). If His heart is our heart, we'll care about the same people Jesus cared about.
- Consider your own life. You believed the gospel because someone cared enough about you to share it with you.
- Jesus was sent to bring light, and His light comes into the world through the lives and lips of His people. Every Jesus follower has been sent to share His love with the world.
- The desire to share in the mission comes from our growing relationship with the Father.
- When we're investing in our relationship with God and growing in intimacy, we'll naturally want to share what God is doing in our lives with the people around us—both locally and globally.

CONSIDERATIONS

Your group will likely contain people with one or both of the following feelings towards God's mission.

1. Those who feel the mission isn't for them. They may not put it exactly that way, but many in the church live as though engaging in God's mission requires a special calling to be a missionary, pastor, or evangelist. They haven't grasped that God's call to share in the mission is Christianity 101. You will want to gently push back against this assumption. The Bible contains many commands to be on mission. To be a Jesus follower is to be on mission with Jesus.

2. Those who feel overwhelmed and don't know where to begin. Everywhere we look there are people in need of Jesus. Many people see the sheer magnitude of the need and never engage the mission because they're so overwhelmed by the size. The good news is that God isn't calling us to do everything; He's calling us to do something. None of us can complete God's mission on our own. That's why the mission was given to the entire church.

NOTES

_____

_____

_____

_____

_____

_____

_____

_____

_____

_____

_____

_____

BIG IDEA

We share in God's mission out of the overflow of our relationship with Him.

KEY SCRIPTURES

Luke 4:42-43

CONVERSATION HELPS

- As you follow Jesus, what is on His heart will be on your heart. As you invest in your relationship with Him, you'll care about the world.
- Jesus was concerned about the expanse of His kingdom—His sovereign activity in the world resulting in people being in right relationship with Him.
- The kingdom is continually expanding as the mission goes forward.
- God is at work all over the world, and He brought us into a relationship to join Him in that work. We accept the invitation and allow Him to work through us.
- The apathy and disinterest of Christians is the greatest obstacle to the kingdom expanding. In order for the kingdom to expand, we must overcome our own selfishness.
- As we saw in earlier sessions, we become less selfish the more that we invest in a love relationship with the Father.
- Jesus was tempted like we are, this likely includes a temptation towards apathy, but the Scriptures continually show Jesus stealing away to be alone with the Father. This fueled His desire to expand God's kingdom.
- We all bear the responsibility to share in God's mission locally and globally.

CONSIDERATIONS

Help people get a handle on where they can share in the mission locally and globally. A good place to begin is by answering the following questions:

- **What do you do?** What do you do for a living, and how could God use your profession to bring His light into the world? You are not in your career by accident. Don't believe the lie that only ministers and other "professional" Christians share in the mission. All of us can bring our vocations to God as an offering.

- **What can you do?** What skills do you have? Management, finance, education, artistic skills? You are naturally gifted at something and should be leveraging those gifts for God's renown. Instead of using your skills to build your own wealth, use them for the kingdom.

- **What do you love doing?** What are your hobbies and interests? Writing, photography, playing sports, listening to music, exercise? God can use interests and affinity to bring you into relationships with people you might never meet otherwise. Some of the people you meet pursuing an interest may not know Jesus. Use your passion to share Him with the world.

NOTES

_____

_____

_____

_____

_____

_____

_____

_____

_____

_____

_____

_____

THE BIG PICTURE

Investing in the three relationships that matter to Jesus allows us to follow Jesus with an unburdened heart.

KEY SCRIPTURES

Mark 1:35

Luke 4:16

Acts 2:42

Luke 19:10

Acts 1:8

CONVERSATION HELPS

Four ways to invest our time

- God Time—time spent daily alone in fellowship with God.
- Gather Time—time spent weekly gathering in worship with your church.
- Group Time—time spent consistenly in community with a small group from your church.
- Go Time—time spent annually going on mission with God cross-culturally.

You start investing in the relationships Jesus walked in by embracing the 5 Percent Life.

- One percent of your day invested in God Time. That means 15 minutes of enjoying fellowship with God through His Word and prayer.
- One percent of your week invested in Gather Time. That means about an hour and a half spent in worship gathered together with your church.
- One percent of your month invested in Group Time. That means about seven hours each month spent in community with people you care about and who care about you. That's seven hours of doing life together.
- Two percent of your year invested in Go Time. That means approximately seven days each year where you intentionally share in God's mission through serving

opportunities, going on trips, and leveraging your jobs, skills, and passions locally and/or globally.

- Remember the 5 Percent Life is simply a starting point. It's not the target. The target is to faithfully follow Jesus as defined by the three relationships we've identified with God, one another, and the world. .

CONSIDERATIONS

Because we all have a tendency to make following Jesus about what we know and what we do, it can be easy to turn the 5 percent life—a guide to help you invest in relationships—into a list of to-dos that actually pull you away from God.

Help your group to see that this isn't a list of things to do but a series of relationships to invest in. Following the 5 percent life isn't a box to check, they're simply proven means to increase depth and intimacy with the Father.

NOTES

_____

_____

_____

_____

_____

_____

_____

_____

_____

_____

_____

_____

_____

_____

_____

IS YOUR HEART OPEN TO WHERE GOD WANTS TO LEAD YOU?

While on a trip to the Himalayas, David Platt saw such staggering physical and spiritual needs that it changed the course of his life. Now he's inviting you on a similar journey. It begins with the beauty of breathtaking heights, but quickly winds down into heartbreaking depths. As you travel with David through these mountain villages and the Gospel of Luke, you will encounter some difficult questions, but it's the answers that may challenge you the most.

a small-group experience

SOMETHING NEEDS TO CHANGE

A Call to Make Your Life Count in a World of Urgent Need

DAVID PLATT

LifeWay

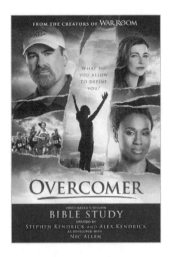

OVERCOMER
by Alex Kendrick & Stephen Kendrick

Learn to define yourself by what God says about you.

LEADER KIT 005817740
BIBLE STUDY BOOK 005814003

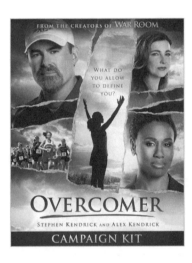

OVERCOMER CHURCH CAMPAIGN KIT
by Alex Kendrick & Stephen Kendrick

Host a special series around *OVERCOMER*. Includes *Leader Kit*, sermon outlines, and other resources to equip your church.

CHURCH CAMPAIGN KIT 005818322

LifeWay
GROUPS
MINISTRY

LifeWay.com | 800.458.2772

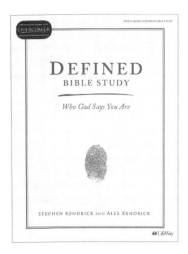

DEFINED
by Alex Kendrick & Stephen Kendrick

Know who you are in Christ and understand how your identity in Christ shapes your life.

LEADER KIT 005817742
BIBLE STUDY BOOK 005802010

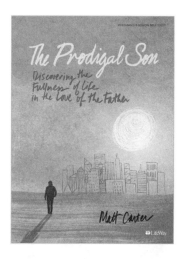

THE PRODIGAL SON
by Matt Carter

Discover the best life is found in the love of your Father.

LEADER KIT 006104396
BIBLE STUDY BOOK 006104395

HELP MY UNBELIEF
by Barnabas Piper

Discover the God who not only desires our belief but actually welcomes our curiosity.

LEADER KIT 005816358
BIBLE STUDY BOOK 005816357

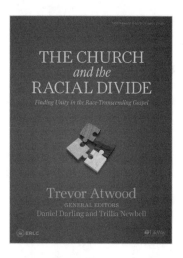

THE CHURCH AND THE RACIAL DIVIDE
by Trevor Atwood and The Ethics & Religious Liberty Commission

See how the gospel affects issues of race and culture, and equip your group to take positive action.

LEADER KIT 005820933
BIBLE STUDY BOOK 005820932